POLICY REPRESENTATION IN WESTERN DEMOCRACIES

Policy Representation
in Western Democracies

Warren E. Miller
Roy Pierce
Jacques Thomassen
Richard Herrera
Sören Holmberg
Peter Esaiasson
Bernhard Wessels

OXFORD

UNIVERSITY PRESS

OXFORD
UNIVERSITY PRESS

Great Clarendon Street, Oxford OX2 6DP

Oxford University Press is a department of the University of Oxford.
It furthers the University's objective of excellence in research, scholarship,
and education by publishing worldwide in

Oxford New York

Athens Auckland Bangkok Bogotá Buenos Aires Calcutta
Cape Town Chennai Dar es Salaam Delhi Florence Hong Kong Istanbul
Karachi Kuala Lumpur Madrid Melbourne Mexico City Mumbai
Nairobi Paris São Paulo Singapore Taipei Tokyo Toronto Warsaw

and associated companies in Berlin Ibadan

Oxford is a registered trade mark of Oxford University Press
in the UK and certain other countries

Published in the United States
by Oxford University Press Inc., New York

British Library Cataloguing in Publication Data

Data available

Library of Congress Cataloging-in-Publication Data

Policy representation in Western democracies / Warren E. Miller . . .
[et al.].
Includes index.
1. Representative government and representation—United States.
2. Representative government and representation—Europe.
3. Comparative government. I. Miller, Warren E. (Warren Edward),
1924– .
JK271.P5588 1999   321.8′09182′1—dc21   99–25727
ISBN 0–19–829570–7

1 3 5 7 9 10 8 6 4 2

Typeset by Graphicraft Limited, Hong Kong
Printed in Great Britain
on acid-free paper by
Biddles Ltd
Guildford and King's Lynn

Preface

This book is a tribute to Warren E. Miller. It is very sad that he did not live to see this book in print, while in so many ways it is his book. It would not have been possible without his guidance and inspiration. As he himself sketches out in the introductory chapter, the intellectual roots of this book go back to the 1950s when Warren Miller and Donald E. Stokes conducted a novel study of popular representation in the United States Congress by coupling interview materials drawn from voters in a sample of congressional districts with counterpart information from interviews with their representatives in Washington, along with roll-call votes cast by those representatives on behalf of their districts. The first results of the study were reported in an APSR-article *Constituency Influence in Congress*, published in 1963. This was and still is one of the most cited articles in political science. It also became the source of inspiration for many studies of political representation in the following decades both in and outside the United States.

The role Warren Miller has played in the development of comparative political research is tremendous. His role in building a program of national election studies modelled after the Michigan studies in many countries is widely known. Perhaps less known is his vital role in setting up a series of studies of political representation in Western Europe, in particular in the Netherlands and Sweden. His personal friendship with Bo Särlvik enabled him to take part in the first Swedish representation study in the 1960s. A visiting professorship in the Netherlands in the early seventies was the ideal setting for playing a similar role in that country as well. In the same period, representation studies were conducted in France, West-Germany, and Italy. Book-length reports were published on the studies in each of these countries. However, what was missing was a really comparative study taking institutional differences between countries into account. Although Warren and some of us started to discuss the possibility of a really comparative study as early as the mid-seventies, it took us twenty more years to realise this plan.

The length of time it took to finish this study is reflected in both the data sources and the authorship of this book. The book is partly based on the data that was collected in the late sixties and early seventies as part of Warren's effort to establish a comparative program of representation studies. However, as far as data from later replications of the original study design were available, we used these as well. The long journey of the project is also reflected in the authorship. For two of us, Soren Holmberg and Jacques Thomassen, this book marks the beginning and the end of our intellectual relationship and personal friendship with Warren. We both started our academic careers by writing a dissertation on the basis of the original representation study in Sweden and the Netherlands respectively. Roy Pierce worked with Philip Converse on Political Representation in France for almost two decades, implementing the original Miller and Stokes model in France. Peter Esaiasson, Richard Herrera, and Bernhard Wessels not only represent a younger generation of scholars, but also a remarkable renaissance of empirical research on political representation on both sides of the Atlantic. For all of us, Warren's leadership and intellectual stimulation has been invaluable. In this manuscript as in numerous others, whether bearing his name as an author or not, his intellectual and personal influence is deeply rooted. With proud and gratitude we dedicate this book to the memory of Warren E. Miller, an outstanding scholar and a good friend. He will not be forgotten and his work will live on.

May 1999

Peter Esaiasson, Göteborg
Richard Herrera, Phoenix
Sören Holmberg, Göteborg
Roy Pierce, Ann Arbor
Jacques Thomassen, Enschede
Bernhard Wessels, Berlin

Contents

List of Contributors

WARREN MILLER was Regents Professor of Political Science, Arizona State University. He was a Principal Investigator for the American National Election Studies for 47 years and in that time also was president of the American Political Science Association, recipient of the Association's Frank J. Goodnow Award for Distinguished Service to the Profession of Political Science, founder of the InterUniversity Consortium for Political and Social Research, founder of the Centre for Political Studies at the University of Michigan, founder of the Social Science History Association, and renowned author of countless articles and books on the electoral process. He was one of four co-authors of *The American Voter* (1960), a landmark work on voting behaviour and most recently, was co-author of *The New American Voter* (1996), advancing that earlier work into contemporary politics. He received an honorary degree from the University of Goteborg, elected to the Norwegian Academy of Science and Letters, honoured by the American Political Science Association Section on Elections, Public Opinion and Voting Behaviour through the creation of the Warren E. Miller Award for Intellectual Accomplishment and Service and was the recipient in 1995, and was an active promoter of electoral voting research in the Netherlands, Norway, Sweden, Germany, Japan, and Great Britain.

ROY PIERCE is Professor Emeritus of Political Science and Faculty Associate Emeritus of the Centre for Political Studies of the University of Michigan. His most recent books include *Presidential Elections in France and the United States* (1995) and, with Philip E. Converse, the Woodrow Wilson Prize-winning *Political Representation in France* (1986). His special interest is mass–elite relations, and he has contributed some 40 chapters and articles to other books and scholarly journals.

JACQUES THOMASSEN is Professor of Political Science at the University of Twente. He is a member of the Royal Netherlands Academy of Arts and Sciences. Among his latest publications is *Political Representation and Legitimacy in the European Union* (Oxford: Oxford University Press, 1999) which he co-edited with Hermann Schmitt.

RICHARD HERRERA is Associate Professor of Political Science at Arizona State University. His published articles about political representation have appeared in *Journal of Politics*, *Party Politics*, *Political Science Quarterly*, *Political Studies*, and *Public Opinion Quarterly*.

SÖREN HOLMBERG is Professor of Political Science and Election Research at Goteborg University. Since 1979 he has been the leader of the Swedish Election Studies Program. He is also a co-leader of the Som-Institute. Among his publications in English are: *The Political System Matters* (1988, co-authored with Donald Granberg), and *Representation from Above* (1996, co-authored with Peter Esaiasson).

PETER ESAIASSON is Professor of Political Science at Göteborg University. Among his publications in English are: *Representation from Above* (1996, co-authored with Sören Holmberg) and *Beyond Westminster and Congress: The Nordic Experience* (1999, co-editor).

BERNHARD WESSELS is Senior Fellow at the Wissenschaftszentrum Berlin für Sozialforschung (WZB), research unit 'Institutions and Social Change'. He has been the principle investigator of studies of German Bundestag members and candidates since 1988, and has currently co-ordinated a European-wide, cross-national parliamentary survey on political representation in Europe. He has published widely on German political elites, political representation, interest groups, electoral behaviour, and political sociology, including the books *Konfliktpotentiale und Konsenssstrategien* (co-ed. 1989), *Abgeordnete und Bürger* (1990), *Erosion des Wachstumsparadigmas: Neue Konfliktstrukturen im politischen System der Bundesrepublik?* (1991), *Politische Klasse und politische Institutionen* (co-ed. 1991), *Parlament und Gesellschaft* (co-ed. 1993), *Verbände in vergleichender Perspektive* (co-ed. 1997), *The European Parliament, National Parliaments, and European Integration* (co-ed. 1999).

Abbreviations

ANES	American National Election Study
APSA	American Political Science Association
CDA	Christian Democratic Appeal
CDS	Convention Delegate Study
CDU/CSU	Christian Democratic Union/Christian Social Union
D66	Democrats 1966
DFG	Deutsche Forschungsgemeinschaft
ECPR	European Consortium for Political Research
FDP	Free Democratic Party
FGDS	Federation of the Democratic and Socialist Left
GOP	Grand Old Party
ICPSR	InterUniversity Consortium for Political and Social Research
NSF	National Science Foundation
PCF	Parti Communiste Français (French Communist Party)
PR	Proportional representation
SPD	Social Democratic Party
UNR	Union for the New Republic
WZB	Wissenschaftszentrum Berlin

1

Elite–Mass Linkages in
Representative Democracy
Introduction

Warren E. Miller

The seven chapters of this book bring partial closure to an effort begun more than thirty years ago. The chapters present six very different perspectives on the topic of policy representation in the national legislative institutions of five North Atlantic democracies. The chapters are the product of a long overdue decision to capitalize on an intellectual initiative taken in the 1960s by this author and several colleagues then associated with the Political Behavior Program of the University of Michigan's Survey Research Center. The next few pages sketch the historical context in which this book has been written and from which it should be viewed.

The research agenda of the Political Behavior Program (later to become the Center for Political Studies) originated in the Michigan studies of national presidential and congressional elections in the United States. From an early date, however, interest expressed by colleagues in other countries encouraged the Michigan people to enter into collaborative arrangements abroad. One of the earliest and most rewarding of these resulted in the pioneering work of Butler and Stokes that produced *Political Change in Britain* (David Butler and Donald Stokes, London: MacMillan, 1969). Less well known is the fact that Stokes, in particular, was at the same time pursuing a replication of one of the best publicized unpublished books in modern political science (Miller and Stokes, *Representation in the United States Congress*, Prentice-Hall, forthcoming). The latter volume was to have been a major report on a study of policy representation in the United States Congress. That study had employed a unique design for data collection focused on the intersection between the policy preferences of the *constituents* of members of Congress and the policy preferences—and legislative acts—of the *congressional members* themselves.

The sheer outline of the study alone was enough to spark the imagination of colleagues. Those already committed to the use of the survey research for the study of elections easily recognized the opportunity to contribute hitherto unavailable evidence to the study of the processes of representation. With the occasional adaptation of sampling designs, studies of the mass electorate could become the foundation for studies of the interaction between mass politics and elite government. Inasmuch as an increasing number of national election studies had been completed or were planned in a number of countries, it was as easy as it was exciting to visualize the emergence of a massive array of data crafted to facilitate the comparative study of cross-national similarities and differences in the actual operation of national systems of democratic self-government.

Members of the Michigan group shared an understanding that the major differences among the social science disciplines originate in the institutions that preoccupy each discipline; and that within each discipline the human phenomena that need to be understood are those shaped by variations in institutional arrangements. In turn, variance in institutional arrangements pertaining to the governing of nations can be satisfied, at least in the abstract, by studying synchronic variations across national boundaries in the current era, or by diachronic studies of institutional changes occurring through time in the institutions of single nations.

We pursued both alternatives. The Michigan election studies became the National Election Studies and now span four decades. During this time, some of us joined forces with like-minded historians and were part of the midwifery that produced the Social Science History Association.

Other energies went into the creation of a multinational base for the study of contemporary interactions between political masses and elites. The Political Behavior Program was transformed into the Center for Political Studies when, in 1970, we were encouraged by the Ford Foundation to facilitate technology transfer to political science in Latin America. There we carried our commitment to comparative politics by helping to create a programme for graduate training in Brazil, as well as by using a study of mass–elite relationships in Brazil as a vehicle for exemplary research.

From other venues, Philip Converse's long-standing interest in French politics ultimately produced the magnificent volume *Political Representation in France* (Cambridge, Mass.: Harvard, 1986) co-authored with Roy Pierce— but more about him in a moment. Converse subsequently collaborated with John Maisel in launching the Canadian studies. Thanks to the interests of Max Kaase, Hans-Dieter Klingemann, and Rudolph Wildenmann an active collaboration with Michigan began that is still sustained in Mannheim through Hermann Schmitt and through Bernhard Wessels in Berlin.

At the turn of the decade, Aage Clausen and I ventured to Göteborg to participate in the Swedish representation study. It was directed by Bo Särlvik with the assistance of Olof Petersson, and by Sören Holmberg, who has since succeeded Särlvik as director of the many-faceted Götenborg media and election studies. I also drew on a friendship developed in the Netherlands with Philip Stouthard when we both taught at an early ECPR summer school in Amsterdam. With the enthusiastic support of Hans Daalder and the assistance of Felix Huencks, Jacques Hagenaars, and Jacques Thomassen, a study of mass–elite linkages in the Netherlands was undertaken as a sequel to earlier work by Daalder on the Dutch Second Chamber.

After a number of false starts elsewhere in South America, our largest institutional commitment was made in Brazil. Converse and Peter McDonough managed a striking success in completing a data collection from most of the Brazilian electorate and scores of politically relevant elites in the midst of 'the reign of the generals' in the early 1970s. Without knowingly amplifying the meaning of cultural imperialism, our personal and professional networks had taken colleagues from the Center for Political Studies to Australia, Canada, Germany, India, Italy, and Japan, as well as Britain, France, the Netherlands, and Sweden.

Each new study was, as in the American case, a measured success in creating an extraordinary assemblage of data, both micro- and macro-, and both public record and those generated specifically for research. The data documented the structures and the processes connecting one subset of a nation's rulers with a representative sample of the ruled. In many countries the prodigious efforts devoted to the project produced one or more major monographic reports or books.

Nevertheless, the 'parent' study resulted in no more than a handful of journal articles, early proclaiming the forthcomingness of the major analysis by Miller and Stokes, *Representation in the United States Congress*. The methodological problems related to cross-level analysis in the study of congressional representation were new to us; we also had our first experience with panel data; and we faced a host of measurement tasks that were daunting if manageable. Moreover, distractions from other challenges (such as the British election study and the organization of the ICPSR, both in 1962) overwhelmed us. And so, a project that we thought would revolutionize the study of representation died aborning, uncompleted and unpublished.

Our singular failure to complete the Miller–Stokes study of representation in the United States foreshadowed an analogous failure on the international front. Neither the Michigan group nor our colleagues in other countries could assemble the resources needed to combine two or more national efforts in a truly comparative, cross-national analytic mode.

The pervasiveness of our frustration with the absence of support, public or private, for the extraordinary costs of carrying out cross-national research was reflected in a rather unique international research conference hosted by the Center for Political Studies in 1977. The primary goal of the conference, funded by joint grants from the German Deutsche Forschungsgemeinschaft and the American National Science Foundation, was 'to provide funding agencies with a concrete catalogue of recommendations aimed at improving the state of cross-national research'. Ten recommendations of the conference ranged from urging national funding agencies (such as the DFG and the NSF) to coordinate the timing of their proposal reviews for joint or multinational projects, to detailing the need for the inevitable costs of coordinating the activities of individual researchers or research groups from different institutions separated by international if not intercontinental distances (Max Kaase and Warren E. Miller, 'Report on a Conference on Cross-national Research in the Social Sciences', 1977). This effort to counter the negative images of 'junketing scholars' and 'safari research' was not manifestly successful. Funds were not to be found for realizing the analytic phase of our cross-national efforts to study policy representation in national legislatures.

It is nevertheless true that in recent years other projects with similarly ambitious efforts to encompass international coverage have been famously successful. Most recently the Kaase–Newton–Scarbrough leadership of the Beliefs in Government project brought almost sixty scholars together to make a prodigious contribution to the professional literature on comparative politics (Max Kaase, Kenneth Newton, and Elinor Scarbrough, *Beliefs in Government*, Oxford University Press, 1995). Barnes and Jennings from the Center for Political Studies were among the score of research scholars who played major roles in the five-nation study of *Political Action* (Samuel Barnes, Max Kaase, et al., *Political Action*, Beverly Hills: Sage, 1979) and its sequel, M. Kent Jennings and Jan van Deth, *Continuities in Political Action* (Berlin: de Gruyters, 1989). And under the intellectual leadership of Ronald Inglehart of Michigan, the Eurobarometers are now a centrepiece for much cross-national analysis of European political opinion. None the less, very few of the results from the early 'Representation' studies of the 1960s or 1970s found their way to the professional literature, and none of those as comparative, cross-national analysis.

This is not to suggest that the mass–elite linkage problem went untended in various national settings. As Bernhard Wessels notes in Chapter 7, five of the 'old studies' (from France, the Netherlands, Sweden, and the United States) are joined in this volume by another five studies (and with the addition of Germany) from the 1980s. Sweden, in particular, has taken to the initial idea with a vengeance and now, as a matter of virtual routine, Sören Holmberg oversees studies of voters, Riksdagsmen, and journalists. In addition, Holmberg conducts content analyses of the mass media along with analyses of party platforms on the occasion of each national election. In the United States the Center for Political Studies has substituted delegates to the parties' presidential nominating conventions for congressional candidates to represent national political elites and has maintained data collections from 1972 to 1992. In Europe some of the interest in mass–elite linkages through the processes of representation has been refocused on the elections of the European parliament with major contributions from two of this volume's authors, Bernhard Wessels and Jacques Thomassen. Such studies will, of course, by the very nature of their subject-matter invite cross-national analysis and comparison.

Recognizing the sustained, widespread interest in the study of representation, Bernhard Wessels and colleagues at the Science Centre in Berlin invited a number of research scholars to a conference on representation at the Centre in 1989. One outcome of the conference was the decision taken by the authors of this volume to see whether some of the many relevant national studies could be assembled for a truly comparative, cross-national analytic exercise without additional data collection. As with the shared enthusiasm of twenty years earlier, at first there seemed to be a 'will' with no apparent 'way'. In the absence of even 'seed grant' funding for travel, research assistance, or the conferences needed for planning, the seven of us developed a mode of self-support that has proved moderately viable. With some rare exceptions, such as provided twice by the Berlin Science Centre, each participant, in turn, accepted responsibility to provide his own international travel and to provide 'local expenses' for the others on the occasion of our annual assemblies. With generous support from the Berlin Science Center, and some individual initiative and support from home institutions, we managed six meetings—two in Berlin; one in Göteborg, Sweden; one in Ann Arbor, Michigan; one in Tempe, Arizona; and one in Enschede, the Netherlands.

Apart from the two or three days spent together each year, our joint enterprise is the work of individual scholarship. Once we had agreed that each chapter would be comparative and would present analyses involving two or more countries, each author pursued his own interests. Of course, each meeting of the group brought suggestions—usually gentle—for amending the thrust, or the drift, of this or that argument. E-mail has also facilitated many bilateral exchanges. Most important of all, each member of the group generously supplied others with national data to be joined in an international data pool. However, the question of whether we would ever really have a 'book' was answered variously from time to time, occasionally with near despair at the barren prospect of producing something that belonged between only two covers.

A saving grace for this problem is suggested by the bibliographies that have been assembled to accompany the chapters. As this set of references indicates, the very proliferation of analytic approaches, methods, technique, and theoretical perspectives that has occurred over the past thirty years in the course of organizing the various data collections on which the book rests has made evident the relevance of a host of topics that can be subsumed under the theme of representation. Nevertheless, it remains true that the following chapters are not a sustained treatment of the themes conventionally central to the literature on representation. Indeed, the assemblage of chapters is notable for their diversity. Moreover, no one of the authors would propose that his chapter presents a definitive last word on his topic.

The merit of this collection of essays and analyses is to be found in the imaginative and suggestive ideas introduced in each chapter. Their relevance to conventional ways of thinking about both the political and the governmental dimensions of policy representation is clear, but each set of arguments opens new avenues of inquiry. This joint effort was not motivated by any expressed desire to be iconoclastic. Nor was a drive to be unique or unorthodox evident in our many discussions. Nevertheless, each of the six substantive chapters introduces an interesting line for further speculation and inquiry.

We open the volume with a provocative and persuasive critique of the party representation model of mass–elite relationships. Roy Pierce introduces a very useful measure, Pierce's Q, to assess the match between the issue preferences of voters and parties. The Pierce analysis sharply questions the extent to which multiple-party systems in fact promote party–voter linkages on issues of public policy more effectively than does the American two-party system. In addition to offering a fresh perspective on political systems based on a variety of configurations of political parties, this chapter suggests that 'the small and simple US two-party system produces a higher incidence of multiple party– voter issue linkages than the large and complex multi-party systems do'.

In Chapter 3, Jacques Thomassen explores in some detail one possible set of explanations for the failure of the multi-party systems suggested by Pierce. In a direct examination of the received wisdom concerning the role of social structure in shaping national party issue politics, Thomassen finds weak evidence, at best, of linkages between social class cleavages and policy preferences. He concludes that 'the two major models of political representation, the responsible party model and the delegate model, can only be effective as models of linkage if the political elite and the mass public share a common one-dimensional belief system'.

Next, the foundations essential for sharing belief systems are explored by Richard Herrera's analysis of 'The Language of Politics'. He describes a search for the shared understandings of ideological terminology that would enable political masses to follow the arguments of political elites. After making allowances for those ordinary citizens who are least involved in politics, Herrera concludes that 'past studies may have overemphasized constraint and sophist-ication as [necessary] criteria for political engagement by the mass citizenry. Indeed, given those [past] studies, the results presented here indicate a remarkably informed electorate. [The mass citizenry] appear to be *able* to follow the discourse of politics, whether they choose to or not.'

Continuing the focus on similarities and differences in mass and elite policy preferences, Sören Holmberg builds on early work by the Norwegian sociologist Johan Galtung. The classic differences (and progression implicit) in the AJUS shapes of curves representing distributions of policy preferences are given added meaning in his speculation about the relationship between leaders and their constituents. After comparing distributions of mass and elite opinions in all five countries, Holmberg also concludes that 'it is evident that the similarities [among countries] are more apparent than the differences . . . policy congruence between voters and leaders does not tend to be higher in systems where the responsible party model is the model of governance (Sweden, Germany, and the Netherlands) than in the USA and France where more mixed systems of governance are used.'

Peter Esaiasson brings the comparative study of systems of representation back to the Miller–Stokes interest in the constituency. Against the evidence that 'the existence of geographically based representation is a well established truth in single-member district systems like Britain and the USA' Esaiasson concludes that such is not the case in Sweden or Germany. The evidence suggests that, as in Israel and the Netherlands, there are constituency-based, geographical differences in voter preferences in both Sweden and Germany. However, where one finds geographically based variations in voters' policy views, in neither country does the representation system reflect these voter differences.

Evidence of systemic differences across the five countries is most strik-ing in Bernhard Wessels's concluding chapter. Emphasizing the continuum extending from majoritarian to proportional decision rules governing elec-tion outcomes, Wessels confirms related differences in median-voter and party-voter effects. In this chapter the importance of mass–elite con-gruence in issue or policy representation is established as a part of the larger comparative literature on representation. Indeed, the context for all six pieces of empirical analysis is conveyed through appropriate references to classic works extending from Eulau and Prewitt (1973) through Achen (1977) and Lijphart (1991) to the most recent works of the six major authors of this volume.

REFERENCES

Achen, Christopher, H. (1977), 'Measuring Representation: Perils of the Correlation Coefficient', *American Journal of Political Science*, 21: 805–15.

Barnes, Samuel and Kaase, Max (eds.) (1979), *Political Action* (London: Sage Publications).

Butler, David and Stokes, Donald E. (1969), *Political Change in Britain* (New York: St. Martin's Press).

Converse, Philip E., and Pierce, Roy (1986), *Political Representation in France* (Cambridge, Mass.: Harvard University Press).

Eulau, Heinz and Prewitt, Kenneth (1973), *Labyrinths of Democracy: Adaptations, Linkages, Representation and Policies in Urban Politics* (New York: Bobbs-Merrill Co.).

Jennings, M. Kent and van Deth, Jan W. et al. (1989), *Continuities in Political Action* (Berlin: Walter de Gruyter).

Lijphart, Arend (1991), 'Constitutional Choices for New Democracies', *Journal of Democracy*, 2: 72–84.

Kaase, Max and Newton, Kenneth (1995), *Beliefs in Government* (England: Oxford University Press).

2

Mass–Elite Issue Linkages
and the Responsible Party Model
of Representation

Roy Pierce

INTRODUCTION

The purposes of this chapter are twofold: to investigate to what extent the behaviour of the individual in the mass electorates of five political systems offers empirical support for the responsible party model of representation; and to determine how any such measurable support varies with regard to political system type, issue domain, and party type.

The basic properties of the responsible party model have been set forth periodically in one form or another at least since the mid-1940s, so it is unnecessary to reproduce them here in any detail. The key points are as follows: (1) that voters have various packages of issue positions; (2) that voters compare their positions with those presented (more or less consistently and uniformly throughout the entire electorate) by the competing political parties; (3) that voters vote for the party whose issue package most closely resembles their own; and (4) that the elected officials of each party remain united in an effort to enact their issue package into public policy. The first three of these items relate to individual-level electoral behaviour and will be the focus of our analysis.

The responsible party model, it should be noted, reflects 'an intense commitment to a mandate theory of representation' (Converse and Pierce 1986: 706; also 499–501). Parties are regarded as transmission belts for the conversion of popular desires into public policies. To employ a metaphor that gained some currency in the United States after the Republican victories at the House and Senate elections of 1994, the responsible party model posits a kind of contractual relationship between the electorate and the party. The party will honour its promises, which are presumed to match the desires of the voters who supported that party at the polls.

The main alternative to the party model is the constituency-centred model. The constituency-centred model is similar to the responsible party model in that it too rests on a mandate theory of representation, but the two models differ in their designation of the agents that supply and implement the mandate. In the party model, the national electorate conveys instructions to national parties. These in turn carry out those instructions. In the constituency model, the voters of each separate geographic constituency communicate their wishes to the (presumably) single representative elected for that particular constituency. The constituency model assigns to each legislator the task of satisfying the wishes of the voters in a given electoral district (although there is no general agreement as to whether the constituency involved includes all its voters or simply those who voted for the winning candidate).

Stated in those stark terms, the two models naturally constitute ideal types, and few adherents of either one would expect it to occur in unadulterated form in the real world. The responsible party model does not necessarily exclude the possibility of national parties occasionally moving outside their normal programmatic range in order to indulge some strategically important sectoral interest. Similarly, enthusiasts for the constituency model do not have to rule out the possibility for constituency-oriented legislators also displaying broader partisan sympathies. But the two models differ in their ranking of priorities. The responsible party model may allow for occasional attention to special interests, but national party positions, presumed to be those of the party's voters, are paramount. The constituency-centred model does not prohibit the representative from expressing partisan interests, but in any serious conflict between those and constituency opinion, the latter must prevail.

The only political system of which I am aware that comes close to reflecting the constituency-centred model is that of the United States. Indeed, it was precisely because of an alleged over-concentration on disparate constituency interests in the United States that the responsible-party model was presented, in the early post-Second World War period, as a presumably superior alternative. The leading example of the responsible party system at that time was Great Britain, although the southern dominions of Australia and New Zealand fit the bill as well. The political systems of these countries appeared to offer plausible alternatives to the US one because they too were two-party systems operating under plurality rule elections in single-member districts. The main differences between them and the United States were, at that time, greater policy distance between the two major parties and stronger voting discipline by the elected members of parliament. It must be added, however, that no one knew at the time whether any of those countries—Britain, Australia, New Zealand, or the United States—was characterized by mass electoral behaviour of the kind implied by the responsible party model (and set forth in the conditions listed above).

No one raised the question of how the numerous European multi-party systems, based on proportional representation, fit into this scheme of contrasting models of representation. Eventually, these came to be referred to as 'consensual' systems (Lijphart 1984, 1989) or simply 'representational' systems (Powell 1982, 1989), in contradistinction to majoritarian and/or presidential systems. It is evident, however, that whatever other characteristic features they may have, they must be considered closer to the party representation model than to the constituency-centred model for the good and sufficient reason that list systems of proportional representation operate either with few constituencies small enough to satisfy the constituency-centred model or with none at all. In addition to that obvious but key point, the more or less classic multi-party, list system countries are also typified by the party discipline and, often, party distances required or implied by the responsible party model. As in the cases of the Anglo-Saxon democracies referred to above, however, we have little or no information about whether the behaviour of the electorates of these other countries satisfies the requirements of the party representation model.

We cannot remedy that situation for the entire universe of liberal democracies. We can, however, investigate the problem across five countries at various points in time: France in 1967, the Netherlands in 1971–2 and 1989–90, the United States in 1986–7 and 1988, Germany in 1987, and Sweden in 1988. This assortment of countries offers variations along several dimensions that have long been of interest to analysts seeking to fathom the relationships between institutions and behaviour. Two of the countries employ list systems of proportional representation: the Netherlands (which employs no electoral districts) and Sweden (which has 28 districts ranging in size from 3 to 36 seats). Two others use single-member districts (France and the United States), while one of them (Germany) employs both a list system of PR and the single-member district system, although only the list-based element is considered here. All except the United States are multi-party systems. Among those systems, the number of operational parties (for the purposes of our study) ranges from four in Germany to seven in the Netherlands (in 1971–2), including six for Sweden and for the Netherlands (in 1989–90). The numerous French electoral labels of 1967 have been grouped here into five major categories.

This distribution of cases is almost ideal for our purposes. If our objective were to try to establish links between institutional arrangements and behavioural patterns, the small number of cases would prohibit us from doing so. But we are less concerned here with the number of cases than we are with the variety of political systems represented, and on this score we are well served. Furthermore, we have among our cases two presumptive party representation systems (the Netherlands and Sweden), two systems that are difficult to classify a priori (France and Germany), and the presumably constituency-centred United States.

The variety of systems satisfies our needs nicely because we find very little evidence at the level of individual electoral behaviour to support the responsible party model of representation in *any* of the systems investigated. The degree of variation among systems on this score is small indeed. Yet such variation as we do find is both striking and unexpected. The voters in the United States come closest to displaying the kind of behaviour postulated by the model, which is surprising because the United States is normally associated not with the responsible party model but rather with the constituency-centred model!

DATA AND ANALYTICAL PROCEDURE

Our analysis of the linkages between the issue positions of individual voters and the issue positions of the political parties operates along that dimension of the paradigmatic Miller and Stokes (1966: 361) diamond that, following Converse and Pierce (1986: 504), we will call the AB bond. Figure 2.1 reproduces the Miller–Stokes diamond to refresh the reader's memory. In the

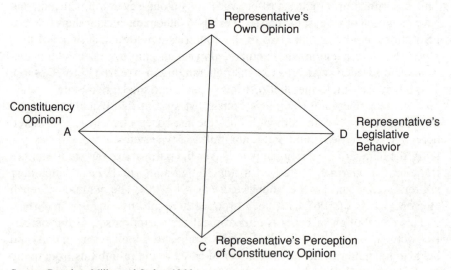

Source: Based on Miller and Stokes 1966.

FIG. 2.1. The Miller–Stokes Diamond

original Miller–Stokes formulation, the A terminal represents the attitude of a constituency, while the B terminal stands for the attitude of a representative. In our analysis, however, A signifies the issue position of an individual voter, while B designates the position on that same issue held by a national political party. We therefore employ individual-level data on the mass side and aggregated data on the elite side to determine whether there is empirical evidence to sustain the responsible party representation model.

On the elite side, the data base consists of aggregated mean issue positions (and their standard deviations), by party, for France in 1967, the Netherlands in 1971 and 1990, Germany in 1987, the United States in 1987 and 1988, and Sweden in 1988. For France, the elite consisted of a district-based national sample of legislative candidates; for Germany, the Netherlands, and Sweden, the elite consisted of the populations of elected deputies. For the United States in 1987 the elite consisted of a national sample of Congress; in 1988 the elite consisted of the delegates to the Democratic and Republican party presidential nominating conventions. The US elites were surveyed by mail; the European elites were surveyed in face-to-face interviews.

On the mass side, we have counterpart individual-level data from national sample surveys conducted in association with the elite surveys from which the aggregated elite data derive. In virtually all cases, except for France, the individual-level data contain mass issue positions measured on scales identical to those employed to ascertain the elite issue positions.[1]

This matching of individual-level issue positions on the mass side against mean party issue positions on the elite side is unusual, if not unique, in this context. Analyses that rest on party representation assumptions normally seek an association between the mean issue positions of each party's elite and the mean positions of each party's voters. There are, however, three weaknesses with that approach.

---

[1] The French data derive from the 1967 surveys on which much of Converse and Pierce (1986) rests. The Swedish data were kindly supplied by Sören Holmberg, of the University of Göteborg. The Dutch elite data were generously provided by Jacques Thomassen, of the University of Twente; the matching Dutch mass data derive from the Dutch Election Study, 1970–3 (ICPSR 7261) and the Dutch Parliamentary Election Study, 1989 (ICPSR 9950). Bernhard Wessels, of the WZB in Berlin, not only supplied the necessary German data but also kindly arranged to have them analysed according to my specifications. Finally, Richard Herrera, of Arizona State University, provided data from a survey of US congressmen he conducted in 1987 as well as relevant analyses he had performed on data from the Convention Delegate Study, 1988 [United States] (ICPSR 6366). The matching US mass data derive from the American National Election Studies for 1986 (ICPSR 8678) and 1988 (ICPSR 9196). The original collectors of these data, including the ICPSR and relevant funding agencies, bear no responsibility for the uses I have made of them or for the inferences I have derived from them.

The first weakness is that mean mass issue positions and mean elite issue positions are not conceptually analogous. The voters for a given party do not constitute an operating entity in the way that a party's elites do—particularly the party's representatives in parliament. Consequently, the average position of a party's elite on some issue scale means something very different from that of the party's voters on the same scale. A parliamentary party is a real group, with regular patterns of communication and decision-making capacity. The mean issue position of the deputies of a given party is potentially convertible into a policy. In that sense, it is quite reasonable to work with elite means, particularly in countries which employ list systems of proportional representation and are characterized by disciplined parties.

The voters for a particular party, however, have no such collective existence. Their mean score on an issue has no reality. Rather, it is an abstraction, an arithmetical expression of a central tendency of the numerous individual issue positions of a party's voters. Neither individually nor collectively, however, do those voters know what that tendency is, nor do they seek to translate it into a policy.

These general considerations concerning the distinction between mass and elite mean issue positions apply directly to the problem at hand. It is particularly appropriate to employ idiosyncratic voter issue positions in a test of the responsible party model of representation because the theory applies to individual voters, each of whom is presumed by the theory to be best served, in representational terms, by some party. The theory relates to parties collectively but to voters individually.

The second weakness of the emphasis on mass mean issue positions follows inevitably from the fact that such means derive from distributions across scales. The dispersion of mass locations on any given issue scale is typically greater than the dispersion of elite positions on the same scale, with the result that similar mass and elite mean positions normally reflect quite different distributions of individual positions. That, in turn, means that while a party's policy on any given issue is likely to reflect a tightly bunched distribution of elite attitudes concerning the issue, there will often be large numbers of that party's voters whose own issue positions will be quite distant both from the mean of all the party's voters and from the party's policy.

Some illustrations of this phenomenon may be drawn from the rich data sets for the Netherlands. In 1971, the mean position on the abortion issue of the voters for the three parties that later merged into the Christian Democratic Appeal, an umbrella religious party, was 3.76 (on a 7-point scale), while the mean position of the CDA deputies was a very similar 3.57. Of those deputies, almost 40 per cent located themselves at 3 or 4 and none placed themselves at the extremes of 1 or 7. Among the voters, however, fewer than

25 per cent placed themselves at 3 or 4 on the same scale, while almost 45 per cent located themselves at the extremes.

That is an extreme case, possibly because of the grouping into a single CDA of what actually were three different parties, or because of the nature of the issue. Later, however, after the CDA had become a real and important entity, we found analogous if less extreme results in connection with the more traditional issue of the distribution of income. In 1990 the mean location of the CDA deputies on income differentials was 3.85, while the CDA voters' mean position was 4.50. Almost 75 per cent of the CDA deputies placed themselves at 3 or 4; while more than 50 per cent of the CDA voters located themselves at positions *other* than 3 or 4. Similarly, almost 75 per cent of the Liberal Party (VVD) deputies placed themselves at 2 or 3 on the same scale, contributing heavily to the party's mean of 2.48, while fewer than 45 per cent of the VVD voters (whose mean location was 3.34) perceived themselves to be at points 2 or 3.

The third weakness in comparing the mean issue positions of party elites with the mean positions of the party's voters is that the mean position of a given party's voters may be close to that of the same party's elite, but it may be even closer to the mean position of the elite of another party. In the Netherlands in 1989–90, for example, the CDA voters and the VVD voters were, on average, closer to the mean position of the Democrats 1966 (D66) deputies on the issue of nuclear power than they were to the deputies of their own parties, while the D66 voters were closer to the mean position of the Labour Party (PvdA) deputies than they were to that of the D66 deputies. In Sweden in 1988, the mean left–right location of the Centre party voters was closer to the mean left–right position of the People's party (Fp) than to that of the Centre party deputies.

The phenomenon of less distance between the mean issue positions of the voters of one party and the elites of another party than between those same voters and the elites of their own party was highlighted in the US context long ago (McCloskey et al. 1960; Kirkpatrick 1976: esp. 297–315) and re-examined more recently by Miller and Jennings (1986: esp. 201–5). It appears, however, to have passed virtually unnoticed in the literature dealing with the multi-party, proportional representation systems of western Europe. Wessels (1991) called attention to several ocurrences of it in the German context, but no one—to my knowledge—has commented on the implications of the phenomenon for the interpretation of mass–elite linkages generally. The dominant mode of analysis for multi-party systems has been to focus only on same-party mass–elite issue proximities.

There are, perhaps, two reasons for this difference in perspectives on the US and the characteristic European political systems, each relating to an important aspect of their institutional arrangements. In contrast to the multi-party European systems, with their numerous choices, the US two-party system lends itself more naturally to either-or considerations.

There is an analogous difference in the domain of the electoral systems. An important characteristic of the European proportional representation systems is that they minimize wasted votes. There is not the sharp distinction between winners and losers that there is in majoritarian, single-member district systems. As a result, there is no obvious institutional incentive to ask, as Converse and Pierce (1986: ch. 19) did for France, whether voters might be better served by losing candidates than by winning candidates. It is apparent, however, that even under list systems of proportional representation, some voters might be better represented on some or most issues by the elites of other parties than they are by the elites of their own. The best way to probe that possibility is to work at the individual level on the mass side of the Miller–Stokes AB bond. That is what we do here.

The basic building blocks on which all of the following analyses rest are sets of individual-level variables, for each country, expressing (for each respondent) which party's position on any given issue was closest to that voter's own position on the same issue. Armed with those sets of Closest Issue-Party variables, we repeatedly ask questions that take the following form: what proportion of the voters for Party A in Country M are closest to that party's position on Issue X? The answers to those questions establish the propensity for the voters in our five countries to vote for the parties they were closest to on the issues tested in their country. That propensity can be expected to vary by country (and its attendant institutional characteristics), by issue domain, and by type of partisan choice.

Another methodological comment must be made at this point. In creating our Closest Issue-Party variables we have not used the raw mass and elite issue position scores but rather the standardized Z scores derived from them. We standardized the mean scores for each party (in each country) by subtracting from each raw party-elite mean the overall raw mean score of all the parties, and then dividing the result by the standard deviation of the overall elite mean. Similarly, we created standardized Z scores for each individual voter, by the same procedure of subtracting from each respondent's raw score the overall mean score of all the mass respondents on the same issue, and then dividing the result by the standard deviation of the overall mass mean. The individual voter's Z score on each issue was compared with the Z scores of all the party elites on the same issue, and the party whose score was least distant from that of the voter, without regard to sign, was registered as the voter's top party for that issue.

We standardize for three reasons. First, by setting the overall mass and elite means for each particular issue to zero and by expressing the individual and partisan scores in terms relative to those means, we emphasize the relational character of those scores. This is precisely what we want for the kind of analysis we are conducting. Before determining which party's position is closest to that of the voter, we order the voters' issue positions relatively and, perhaps even more important, we order the issue positions of the party elites. This permits us to capture the degree of relative congruence there is between voter positions and party positions, as opposed to the degree of absolute congruence that is expressed by the raw scores alone (see Converse and Pierce 1986: 507–10). We are, after all, less interested in knowing which party is least distant from any given voter in an absolute sense than we are in which party, given its location relative to other parties, is closest to that voter, given that voter's location relative to the other voters.

The second reason for standardizing scores is closely related to the first. Indeed, it is to some extent an illustration of the advantage of emphasizing relative over absolute congruence. We have already referred to the numerous cases in which the raw mass mean issue positions of the voters for a given party are closer to the mean issue positions of the elites of another party than they are to the mean position of the elites of the same party. Standardizing scores reduces, although it does not eliminate, those apparent anomalies. For the Netherlands in 1989–90, for example, across the five issues tested for mass–elite congruence, we uncovered twenty-one cases in which that phenomenon occurred. Using standard scores instead of raw scores reduced the number of such cases to thirteen.

Standardizing is particularly helpful when there is a systematic displacement of mass and elite scores due to exaggerated or distorted self-perceptions of one kind or another. Converse and Pierce (1986: 127–33) called attention to the systematic leftward displacement of elite self-perceptions on the left–right scale relative to the self-perceptions of their voters on the same scale. That phenomenon occurs elsewhere as well. In the Netherlands in 1989–90, the mean left–right position of the voters of each of the six parties surveyed was closer to the mean left–right position of the elites of the next party to their right than to the mean position of the elites of their own party. We are, of course, particularly interested in the left–right 'super-issue', but the distortions produced by the raw scores would be a serious obstacle to investigating how the left–right dimension operates in the representational context. Standardizing the scores produces a useful clarification by reducing the number of left–right congruence anomalies from 5 to 1.

Finally, standardization offers the only way to compensate for differences in question wording between mass and elite opinion surveys. In our study, differences in question wording constitute a problem only for France, for which it is, however, quite severe. Only two of the issues cited here were measured by identically worded questions at both the mass and elite levels, although one was the important question dealing with left–right locations (the other related to opinion about incorporating the French army into a European army). Elite opinion on the other issues tested was measured in terms different from those used for the mass sample. Standardizing scores on the resultant mass and elite scales furnished the instrument for solving the problem.[2]

CONTROLLING FOR THE SIZE OF THE PARTY SYSTEM

When we first examined, country by country, the tables cross-tabulating the partisan vote by the party that was closest to the voter on each issue tested, it was immediately apparent that the results would provide little comfort to proponents of the party representation model. The proportions of voters whose position on any given issue was closest to the position of the party for which they voted were just not large enough to suggest that the conditions of the model were being satisfied. More often than not, most of the voters for any given party were closer to the position of some other party on the issue involved than they were to their own party's position. In a surprisingly large proportion of cases, not a single sample voter for a given party (including major parties and not simply minor ones) was closest to that same party on the particular issue being considered!

There was, of course, variation within and between countries with regard to which systems, which issues, and which parties appeared best to satisfy the terms of the model. The largest difference between systems was that between the United States, on the one hand, and all the multi-party systems on the other hand. In the United States, almost 60 per cent of the voters, on the average, were closer to the issue position of the party for which they voted than they were to the other party's position. In the Netherlands (in 1989) and Sweden, two countries whose party and electoral systems would appear to be consonant with the party representation model, barely more than a fourth of the voters were closer to their own parties than to the others.

It is apparent that while this cross-national difference might reflect differing degrees of 'issue packaging' by party, at either the mass or the elite levels or both, some proportion of the difference could simply be the result of the contrast in the number of partisan alternatives offered to the voters in the two-party United States as opposed to the multi-party European systems.

---

[2] As a precaution, we repeated almost the entire set of analyses reported here on the basis of the raw scores in order to determine whether the results would be significantly different depending on which scoring convention we followed. We can assure the reader that that was not the case. See n. 5.

TABLE 2.1. Relationship between the partisan vote and the issue of abortion, Germany, 1987

Electoral choice	Closest party on the abortion issue				
	CDU/CSU	SPD	FDP	Greens	Totals
CDU/CSU	265	73	133	29	500
SPD	229	167	160	82	638
FDP	23	21	24	5	73
Greens	22	37	11	19	89
Total	539	298	328	135	1,300

In the United States, chance alone would produce a 50–50 split among the voters for either party in their location relative to that of their own party on some particular issue. In six-party Sweden, however, equal probability of selection would result in voters being closest to their own party only 17 per cent of the time.

It is, therefore, essential to control for the size of the party system before drawing any conclusions relating to the association between partisan electoral choice and party-voter proximity in issue positions that rest on cross-national analysis. To do this, we devised a formula for the computation of what we will call Pierce's Q.[3] Q may be considered an index of the proportion of cases falling along the diagonal in a symmetrical table, taking account of the maximum number of cases that *could* be in the diagonal and the number of cases that *could be expected* to be in the diagonal on the basis of equal probability of selection.

As an illustration of how Q is computed, Table 2.1 sets out, for Germany, the cross-tabulation between the distribution of the partisan vote and the distribution of the parties that the voters were closest to on the issue of abortion. We observe that there are 475 cases along the diagonal (where the partisan vote and the closest issue party coincide). In the ideal case, where all the voters were closest to the position of their partisan choice on the issue, 1,300 cases would be located on the diagonal. If, however, the voters had no information but the names of four parties, one would expect that one-fourth of the 1,300 cases (325) would fall along the diagonal. The formula for computing Q, therefore, is:

---

[3] Q applies the logic of the measure of agreement *kappa* (Cohen 1960), in easily computable form, to large numbers of respondents.

$$\frac{F_o - F_e}{N - F_e}$$

when F_o is the number of cases observed on the diagonal, F_e is the number of cases expected to appear on the diagonal, and N is the maximum number of cases that can appear on the diagonal (the total number of cases). In the illustration in Table 2.1, $Q = 0.154$.

When Q is positive, that is, when F_o is not less than F_e, it can range from 0 to 1. When F_o is less than F_e, Q is negative. The worst case scenario occurs when the diagonal is totally empty in a two-party system; Q then falls to -1. When the diagonal is empty, but there are more than two parties, Q remains negative but becomes less so as the number of parties increases (and, accordingly, the size of F_e decreases).[4]

RELATIVE VOTER–PARTY ISSUE CONGRUENCE BY COUNTRY AND ISSUE DOMAIN

Table 2.2 sets out the full panoply of Q scores for all the issues tested in the five countries under examination, along with the mean scores for each country and issue domain. For the Netherlands, for which we analysed data at two time periods, we have reported the mean scores for the issues that were included in both studies, but we display the two sets of US scores separately because the nature of the elite base differed in the two US studies. The number and types of issues vary by country, but several important issues are represented in more than one country, including the important ideological measure, which was tested in all five of our countries.

VARIATION BY COUNTRY

The first finding that emerges from considering the country means reported in the last row of Table 2.2 is that while there is considerable variation in those mean scores, none of them is particularly high. Recall that a score of 1 would signify that every voter for each party was closest to that party on the issue in question, while a score of 0 would mean that no more voters

---

[4] When it is inappropriate to compute F_e assuming equal probability of selection, F_e may be computed by taking the marginal distributions into account. To do so, one simply calculates the joint probability of selection for each of the cells on the diagonal, just as one would for all cells when computing Chi square. When F_e is computed in that fashion, Q can reach a maximum of 1, but it can fall below -1, reaching its minimum when F_e is at its maximum but there are no cases on the diagonal.

TABLE 2.2. Mean index scores of voter–party issue matches, by country and issue domain, standardized across national party systems

Issue Domain	France 67		Germany 87		Netherlands 71 & 89[a]		Sweden 88		United States 86		United States 88	
Ideology (0.239)[b]	Left–Right	0.131	Left–Right	0.370	Left–Right	0.084	Left–Right	0.282	Lib–Cons	0.234	Lib–Cons	0.331
Economy (0.107)	Unions	0.056	Unions	0.270	Incomes	0.160	Pub. Sect.	0.176	Services	0.139		
			Jobs	-0.016	Taxes (71)	0.001	Incomes	0.004	Jobs	0.162		
			Econ grth	-0.038			Hlth. ins.	0.170				
			Competition	0.146			6-hour day	0.165				
Society (0.091)	Church schls	0.110	Abortion	0.154	Abortion	0.050	TV adv	0.071	Minorities	0.165	Blacks	0.146
	Education	0.095			Euth. (89)	0.045	Day Care	-0.047			Women	0.123
Environment (0.098)			Environment	0.017	Nuc En. (89)	0.195	Nuc energy	0.070				
			Nuc energy	0.056			Cars	0.150				
Defence and foreign Policy (0.085)	Nuc Stk Fce	-0.030			Defence (71)	0.086	Defence	0.140	Defence	0.125	Defence	0.194
	Foreign Aid	0.000			For aid (71)	0.068			Russia	0.143	Russia	0.101
	Ind for pol	0.021							Cent Amer	0.188		
	Eur army	-0.012										
Participation (0.044)			Law & order	0.207	Law & order (71)	0.109						
			Partcpn	-0.104	Wrkr part (71)	0.017						
			Citzn init	0.059								
			Curb demos	-0.022								
National Means	0.046	N = 8	0.092	N = 12	0.081	N = 10	0.118	N = 10	0.165	N = 7	0.179	N = 5

[a] Mean of both years if no year in parentheses.
[b] Domain means in parentheses.

were in issue accord with their partisan choices than would have occurred by chance. The mean country scores are all much closer to 0 than they are to 1. The highest country mean score is less than 0.20.

The second and even more striking finding is that the top mean score belongs to the United States, regardless of which of the two US analyses we accept. This phenomenon is notable because the United States, with its two-party system and single-member districts, is the prototype of the constituency-centred representational model, while countries like Sweden and the Netherlands, with their multi-party systems operating under list systems of proportional representation, would appear a priori to be better adapted to the responsible party representational model. The prevailing opinion, perhaps best expressed by Dalton (1985), is that multiple parties enhance the likelihood of voters being able to satisfy themselves on multiple issue dimensions simultaneously by making a single partisan choice.

Our analysis suggests, to the contrary, that far from increasing the possibility that voters will find a single party that satisfies them simultaneously on a more or less broad menu of issues, the differentiated issue emphases projected by the elites within multi-party systems may make it *less* likely that they will do so. In the two-party United States, the range of scores reflecting party–voter issue matches is comparatively narrow; no score is lower than 0.100. In the other countries, the gamut is wider and even includes negative scores for Sweden, Germany, and France. Naturally, the pattern of national scores is affected by the issues included in each particular study, and it would not be unreasonable to want to exclude some low scores on the ground that the related issues might not really be visible to much of the electorate. But we find low scores attaching to such issues as income differentials in Sweden, the level of taxation in the Netherlands, and environmental protection in Germany: issues with which one can reasonably assume substantial proportions of the relevant electorates are familiar. If that assumption is anywhere near correct, the figures indicate that even on issues of considerable importance the positions of large proportions of the voters are not as close to the positions of the parties for which they vote as they are to those of other parties.

That phenomenon is particularly evident for France in 1967, whose mean index score is the lowest of all, and close to the chance-alone level of 0. The French party system of that era was characterized by two big electoral blocs separated by a small, inconstant centre. Each of the two big blocs was divided between two major parties of roughly equal electoral strength: the Communists and Socialists on the left, and the Gaullists and Giscardians on the right. Those divisions may have made sense to the political elites who created them, but it is evident that the issue positions of those party elites were not greeted with any systematic echo among the voting public.

VARIATIONS BY ISSUE DOMAIN

Ideology

Table 2.2 groups the distribution of Q scores into six issue domains, reflecting the proportions who voted for the party whose position was closest to their own on the particular issue, controlling for party size. The domain that occupies the head of the list is the generic, ideological 'super-issue' represented in our four European countries by the left–right dimension and in the United States by the liberal–conservative dimension. This broad issue is of particular interest because of the extent to which it may operate as a general organizing concept by which voters orient themselves to the political system apart from consideration of more specific issues. Converse and Pierce (1986: 772–4) hypothesized that the French representative process (in the fullest sense) could be regarded as operating under two forms of popular control: one expressed in terms of specific issues and the other reflected in left–right imagery. The first form implies that voters choose Party A or Party B because they like what those parties stand for on Issue X or Issue Y. The second form signifies that the voters may not know what Party A or Party B stands for on Issue X or Issue Y, but they do know that Party A is leftist and that Party B is rightist and that is enough. Feeling themselves to be leftist or rightist, they vote for the corresponding party and let that party decide what to do on those issues.

The evidence in Table 2.2 indicates that the voters in four of our five countries do indeed practice the loose generic form of electoral control by selecting parties on the basis of ideological distance. The mean Q score for ideological choice is higher by a considerable margin than that for any other issue domain. In each of our countries except the Netherlands, the Q score for ideology is the highest one registered, sometimes by a wide margin. The Dutch exception is probably the result of the electoral prominence in that country of religious outlooks that do not closely correspond with left–right locations. In France, by way of contrast, where the clerical–anticlerical dimension tends to parallel the left–right one, the index figure for ideology registers highest, but it is closely followed by the religion-related issue of state subsidies for church schools.

Economic Issues

After ideology, there is comparatively little variation in the mean levels of the Q scores for four of the remaining five issue domains. Economic issues, social and environmental issues, and defence and foreign policy issues all scored, on the average, close to 0.100. This was unexpected. Given the fact that the left–right dimension normally subsumes certain traditional, class-based economic issues (as well as, in certain countries, religious issues), we had expected economic issues to score less high, on the average, than the over-all ideological domain did, but still discernibly higher than the other issue domains. There are, of course, traces of this: the comparatively high Q scores for three of the four economic issues for Sweden, the high Dutch score for the issue of income differentials, and the impressive German score relating to unions. But in each of those three countries, there were one or more eco-nomic issues that produced scores inconsistent with the hypothesis. It is, of course, possible that plausible country-by-country explanations for each of those anomalies can be found. But such explanations, however persuasive, would do nothing to counter the central point that voters for each party are not uniformly closer to their own party than to the others across the whole spectrum of economic issues.

Social and Environmental Issues

These two issue areas rank on a par with both the economic issues we have just discussed and the defence and foreign policy items. There is little inter-national consistency in this domain. The issue of nuclear energy was tested in three countries, but while it ranks highest among the Dutch items, it regis-ters at comparatively modest levels for Sweden and Germany. Indeed, in Germany the issue of the environment approaches sheer randomness in terms of voter–party issue linkage. Voters in the birthplace of the European green movement are not in any conspicuous fashion selecting parties on the basis of closeness on environmental issues. In Sweden, however, the issue of removing automobiles from central cities placed at a level consistent with those recorded for most economic issues in that country.

Social issues display a similarly mixed pattern. The abortion issue was asso-ciated with electoral choices in Germany at a fairly high level, but Dutch voters appear to have been relatively unmoved by it. In France, the hoary issue of state aid to church schools, which is closely associated with the left–right dimension in that country, registered relatively highly, and so did the more general issue of increased development of education. In the United States, the issues of government aid for minorities and blacks, as well as the issue of women's rights, produced comparatively high levels of vote choice–issue preference congruence.

Defence and Foreign Policy

This domain is represented in only four of our five countries. For France, the Q scores are virtually zero for three of the four items and literally zero for the fourth one. In an era when elite-level political battles were waged in France over relations with the United States, the Soviet Union, and the emergent European Community, French voters appear to have been singularly indifferent to foreign policy issues when making their electoral choices. Swedish voters took defence issues much more seriously in their party selections twenty years later than the French electorate of 1967 had done. For the United States, the index scores for defence and foreign policy issues remain at high levels of the kind characteristic of the other issue domains in that country.

Participatory Issues

The domain of popular participation in decision-making is represented only in our Dutch and German data sets. The items included register at widely varying levels of voter–elite congruence. One issue in this domain, however, that of law and order, appears to have been an important element in electoral choice, particularly in Germany. Other related items, even one referring to curbing demonstrations in Germany—which one would expect to behave similarly to the issue of law and order—register at low or even negative levels.

ABSOLUTE LEVELS OF VOTER–PARTY ISSUE CONGRUENCE, BY COUNTRY AND PARTY TYPE

Our analysis so far indicates strongly that voter–party issue congruence is far from impressive across our selection of political systems. When one controls for the size of the party system, the proportion of voters for any given party that is closest to that party on the various issues we have tested is often not much larger than what chance alone would produce. That proportion varies somewhat from country to country, and from issue to issue, in ways that we have described. There is, however, no evidence to support the notion that many voters approach their electoral choices on the basis of matching their personal packages of issue positions with those offered by the parties. On the contrary, the data so far presented suggest that most voters are likely to be closest to their party of choice only on two or three issues at most.[5]

---

[5] We repeated the analyses underlying Table 2.2 taking the marginal distributions into account. The national mean Q scores were 0.068 for France, 0.088 for Germany, 0.075 for the Netherlands, 0.112 for Sweden, 0.163 for the United States in 1986, and 0.156 for the United States in 1988. The ordering by country remains the same as it appears in Table 2.2, although the two US means are reversed. Ideology remained the most sensitive issue domain (0.226), followed by the economy (0.102), society (0.093), defence and

TABLE 2.3. Mean numbers of voter-party issue matches, by country

Sample	Mean	Standard deviation	No.
Germany (4)[a]	3.82	2.074	1,304
United States 1986 (2)	2.67	1.446	798
Sweden (6)	2.16	1.820	2,338
United States 1988 (2)	2.11	1.180	908
France (5)	1.85	1.686	1,318
Netherlands 1989 (6)	1.30	1.011	1,369
Netherlands 1971 (7)	1.19	1.248	1,261

[a] Number of parties in parentheses.

MEAN LEVELS OF VOTER–PARTY ISSUE MATCHES, BY COUNTRY

There is, of course, no need for us to guess at that figure. It is simple enough to compute on how many issues the party for which each voter cast a ballot was closest to that voter. That sum can range from 0 to a maximum equal to the number of issues tested for each particular sample. The maximum ranged from 5 (for the Netherlands in 1989 and the United States in 1988) to 12 (for Germany in 1987). The mean numbers of voter–party issue matches for our seven samples are reported in Table 2.3.

Those means range from a low of barely more than 1 (for the Netherlands in 1971) to a high of slightly less than 4 (for Germany in 1987). There is a positive correlation between the number of issues tested and the mean number of voter–party issue matches for each sample ($r = 0.65$), so one should be cautious in comparing those means cross-nationally. But the range is narrow, and the mean of the means is barely more than 2. That is a long way from the basic assumptions of the responsible party representation model.

foreign policy (0.085), the environment (0.083), and participation (0.059). The most notable changes were the transformation of all the negative scores reported in Table 2.2 into low positive ones, and the decline in the German Q scores for left–right positioning from 0.370 to 0.299 and for unions from 0.270 to 0.188.

We also repeated the analyses (assuming equal probability of selection for computing Fe) for all the data sets except the German one, using the raw, unstandardized mass and elite issue positions. This did not alter the Q scores in any significant fashion, but had the same effect on their ordering by country and by issue domain that was produced by taking the marginals into account.

TABLE 2.4. Mean number of voter-party issue matches, by type of party

Type of party	Mean	Standard deviation
Leftist (3)[a]	3.34	0.575
Green (3)	2.90	1.719
Conservative (11)	2.42	1.233
Liberal & Centrist (7)	1.78	0.673
Social Democratic (6)	1.42	0.747

[a] Number of parties in parentheses.

MEAN LEVELS OF VOTER–PARTY ISSUE MATCHES, BY PARTY TYPE

To get a sense of the variation in voter–party issue matches by type of party, we have computed the mean number of such matches for five clusters of similar parties that are represented in our samples, without regard to country. Our earlier caution about the inherent problem of making cross-national comparisons concerning mean levels of those matches must, of course, be kept in mind. Moreover, our clusters are unequal in size, as we have only three truly leftist parties and three green parties, as compared with six social democratic parties, seven liberal or centrist parties, and eleven conservative groups. We are not, however, seeking exact measures at this point, but rather only relative orders of magnitude.

The mean scores by type of political party appear in Table 2.4, from which several conclusions emerge. The first, as we might expect, is that the two small clusters of leftist and green parties display the highest mean levels of voter–party issue congruence. Still, the green cluster, as small as it is, has the greatest dispersion of scores of any of our groups of party types, as the comparatively large standard deviation indicates. The high mean for the greens is largely the result of the large number of voter–party issue matches for the German greens.

The second point of some note is that the third most attractive group of parties in terms of issue closeness for their voters is the large and somewhat heterogeneous category of rightist parties. This group also contains a wide range of scores for particular parties, from more than 5 for the German Christian Democratic Union/Christian Social Union (CDU/CSU) to barely more than 1.2 for the Gaullist Union for the New Republic (UNR). Nevertheless, it is of more than passing interest that the conservative parties, on the whole, attract more issue-based support (in the terms in which we have measured it here) than do the social democratic parties, which have long been associated with distinct programmatic emphases.

Indeed, the relatively low level of voter–party issue matches for the social democratic parties constitutes our third general point. The social democrats are outstripped on this measure not only by the conservatives but also by the liberal and centre parties which, in this regard, reveal considerable homogeneity as a group. It is as if the occasional efforts of the big Dutch, German, and Swedish social democratic parties to shed their Marxist heritage and become 'catch-all' parties were not particularly successful in building multiple-issue ties with their voters. But the left-leaning French socialists of the late 1960s were doing even less well than the more moderate social democrats elsewhere. Current programmatic emphases may not, therefore, have been decisive in producing the less than impressive degree of voter–party issue congruence that we find among the social democratic parties in our sample. More fundamental forces seem to have been at work. These were comparatively popular parties everywhere, but their electoral appeal rested only to a limited extent on voter–party issue congruence.

Lastly, it is striking how small a role matching voter–party issue positions appear to have played in the electoral support of both the French Gaullists and leftist-oriented Federation of the Democratic and Socialist Left (FGDS) of the late 1960s. This is entirely consistent with the Converse and Pierce (1986) analysis of the limitations of issue voting in France, although it is expressed in new form here with the sharp contrast between the issue-oriented electorate of the French Communist party and the electorates of the more broadly appealing Gaullists and Socialists.

As our comments on the mean scores reported in Table 2.4 have indicated, there is considerable variation from country to country in the incidence of voter–party issue congruence that is not displayed directly. In order to present that detailed information in maximally accessible fashion, we have reorganized the data on which Table 2.3 and Table 2.4 are based in a way that permits us to array all the parties on a single scale (see figure 2.2).

The placement of the parties on the scale in figure 2.2 reflects the ranking of each party *relative to the other parties in the same country* with regard to the mean number of times the party's voters' positions on issues were closest to those of the party. The scale values are simply the Z scores representing the mean number of voter–party issue matches for each party in each country. In assessing the information in figure 2.2, therefore, it is important to keep two things in mind. First, the scale is essentially an index. It reports only relative scores. Second, when comparing parties directly one must make only intranational comparisons (for the same year), and not cross-national

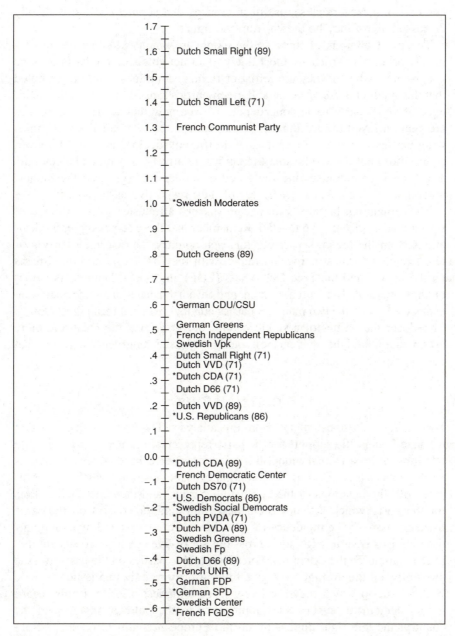

*One of the two largest parties in the country

FIG. 2.2. Index of voter–party issue matches, by party (standardized within national party systems)

comparisons. Nevertheless, useful inferences that supplement those already discussed above may be drawn from the figure.

The most obvious of these is the extent to which extremist (or ideologically oriented) parties are most likely to attract voters on the basis of issue congruence, whether they are leftist or rightist in outlook. Earlier, we noted that the small clusters of leftist and green parties ranked highest in the incidence of voter–party issue congruence. We see now that while those parties are again arrayed toward the top of our scale, so are the small Dutch right-wing parties which are, of course, of a different ideological cast. Moreover, a party does not have to be small to enjoy a relatively like-minded electorate. The French communists and the Swedish moderates registered the highest voter–party issue congruence scores of their respective party systems.

The remaining, largely 'mainstream' parties all cluster within a range of standard scores from +0.6 to −0.6. Remember that these scores represent deviations from the mean, separately for each country. The German party system stretches furthest across its range, with the CDU/CSU and the Greens on the upside and the Free Democrats (FDP) and Social Democrats (SPD) on the downside. The Dutch, French, and Swedish parties are somewhat more compacted, while the two main US parties hug their national mean most closely. The closer the parties of a single country hover around the mean the more evenly distributed the incidence of voter–party issue congruence is across that country's party system.

CONCLUSIONS

Two main conclusions emerge from this analysis. The first conclusion is that we have found little support for the party representation model of mass–elite relations, at least as that model has been interpreted here. Voters do not, as a rule, appear to hold some combination of issue positions which they compare with the positions of the competing parties, and then cast their ballots for the party which satisfies them best (and simultaneously) on the same basket of issues. The incidence of voter issue preferences and matching partisan choices is simply too low across our set of five countries to sustain that interpretation. To the extent that voters respond to parties on the basis of issue proximity, on the average they give high priority to only two issues.

The issue to which they are likely to give highest priority in this regard is the ideological 'super-issue' appropriate to the political imagery of the country: the left–right dimension on the European continent or the liberal–conservative dimension in the United States. Voter–party congruence on more specific issues, even those that are traditionally linked to the ideological dimensions, is much more limited.

This suggests that the kind of control over elected officials that is exercised by the electorate is of the broad generic kind posited by Converse and Pierce (1986) at the level of the legislative district for France and explored further by Huber and Powell (1994) in the form of ideological congruence between the median voter and governing coalitions. Popular control of legislators on specific issues appears to be extremely limited in all of our five sample countries.

The second main conclusion is that to the extent that the party representation model appears to be applicable, it applies most successfully to the two-party United States and much less satisfactorily to the multi-party systems, including those operating under list systems of proportional representation, for which the model has often been suggested to be particularly appropriate. That it is the US party system that makes the United States a better example of the party representation model than the other countries we have examined, and not the US single-member district system, would appear to be supported by the fact that multi-party France, which also operates with single-member districts, ranks so low on the scale of voter–party issue congruence.

It has long been believed that multi-party systems not only make it possible to give political expression to multiple social cleavages, but also provide the voters with opportunities to select from different packages of issue orientations, each of which might be only marginally different from the others. Without in the least challenging the appropriateness of a multi-party system for a society with multiple and deep social cleavages, one must doubt that multi-party systems (at least of the kind examined here) multiply the combinations of issue positions offered to the voters in ways that produce any sizeable mass response. The evidence we have uncovered indicates, to the contrary, that the small and simple US two-party system produces a higher incidence of multiple party–voter issue linkages than the large and complex multi-party systems do.

REFERENCES

Cohen, Jacob (1960), 'A Coefficient of Agreement for Nominal Scales', *Educational and Psychological Measurement*, 20: 37–46.

Converse, Philip E., and Pierce, Roy (1986), *Political Representation in France* (Cambridge, Mass.: Harvard University Press).

Dalton, Russell J. (1985), 'Political Parties and Political Representation: Party Supporters and Party Elites in Nine Nations', *Comparative Political Studies*, 18: 267–99.

Huber, John D., and Powell, G. Bingham Jr. (1994), 'Congruence between Citizens and Policymakers in Two Visions of Liberal Democracy', *World Politics*, 46: 291–326.

Kirkpatrick, Jeane (1976), *The New Presidential Elite: Men and Women in National Politics* (New York: Russell Sage Foundation and the Twentieth Century Fund).

Lijphart, Arend (1984), *Democracies: Patterns of Majoritarian and Consensus Government in Twenty-One Countries* (New Haven: Yale University Press).

—— (1989). 'Democratic Political Systems: Types, Cases, Causes, and Consequences', *Journal of Theoretical Politics*, 1: 33–48.

McClosky, Herbert, Hoffmann, Paul J., and O'Hara, Rosemary (1960), 'Issue Conflict and Consensus among Party Leaders and Followers', *American Political Science Review*, 54: 406–27.

Miller, W. E. and Jennings, M. Kent (1986), *Parties in Transition: A Longitudinal Study of Party Elites and Party Supporters* (New York: Russell Sage Foundation).

—— and Stokes, Donald E. (1966), 'Constituency Influence in Congress', in Angus Campbell, Philip E. Converse, Warren E. Miller, and Donald E. Stokes, *Elections and the Political Order* (New York: John Wiley & Sons).

Powell, G. Bingham Jr. (1982), *Contemporary Democracies: Participation, Stability, and Violence* (Cambridge, Mass.: Harvard University Press).

—— (1989). 'Constitutional Design and Citizen Electoral Control', *Journal of Theoretical Politics*, 1: 107–30.

Wessels, Bernhard (1991), 'Abgeordnete und Bürger', in Hans-Dieter Klingemann, Richard Stöss, and Bernhard Wessels (eds.), *Politische Klasse und politische Institutionen* (Opladen: Westdeutscher Verlag), 325–56.

3

Political Communication between Political Elites and Mass Publics

The Role of Belief Systems

Jacques Thomassen

INTRODUCTION

The (implicit) assumption of many empirical studies of political representation is that 'congruence between the preferences of citizens and the actions of policymakers constitutes a major claim and goal of liberal democracy' (Huber and Powell 1994: 292). Empirical research offers ample evidence that from this perspective liberal democracy in most countries is far from perfect. In many instances the policy views of the members of parliament do not reflect the views of their citizens. In this chapter we shall examine to what extent these many instances form a pattern. Does issue congruence exist for certain kinds of issues and not for others? If so, can we explain why this is the case? We shall argue that in many cases a lack of congruence between elite and mass opinions is due to a difference in belief systems. In general, there is less issue congruence for issues that do not belong to the core of a belief system. In the next section we shall explain the role of belief systems in the main models of political representation. Later, we shall develop and test four hypotheses on the relationship between belief systems and the policy preferences of the mass public and the political elite.

POLITICAL REPRESENTATION AND BELIEF SYSTEMS

According to Converse (1964: 207), belief systems can be defined 'as a configuration of ideas and attitudes in which the elements are bound together by some form of constraint or functional interdependence'. 'Constraint' here suggests the success one might have, given initial knowledge that an individual holds a specific attitude, in predicting that the individual holds certain further ideas and attitudes. It is easy to demonstrate the importance of a functional interdependence of different policy views in the two main theories of political representation or 'models of linkage', the *responsible party model* and the *delegate model*. In the traditional formulation of the responsible party model belief systems or ideologies hardly play a role. The basic requirements of the model are that

(*a*) different political parties present different policy alternatives to the voters,

(*b*) the internal cohesion, or party discipline, of political parties is sufficient to enable them to implement their policy program, and

(*c*) voters vote for the party that is closest to their own policy preferences (Thomassen 1994: 251–2).

If both parties and voters behave according to the above requirements, the (majority of the) electorate enforces a government policy that will be congruent with their own policy views. However, this is not necessarily the case. Even when all voters vote according to their issue positions, the election outcome does not necessarily convey an electoral mandate on particular policy positions. Political parties offer a package deal to the voter; by voting for a particular party, voters vote for the whole package. However, this does not necessarily mean that all voters support all elements of the package. It is still possible that the winning majority represents a minority on each policy domain. Social choice theory seems to demonstrate that the preferences of citizens are almost always collectively uninterpretable if they form more than one dimension (Huber and Powell 1994: 292). Therefore, without further assumptions, a single vote does not convey a mandate with respect to any policy domain. Only when both the policy programmes of political parties and the voters' attitudes are based on the same one-dimensional ideology (Thomassen 1994: 253–4) can an electoral majority be interpreted in an unequivocal way.

Therefore, the effectiveness of the responsible party model depends on the extent to which the policy views of both masses and elites are constrained by a one-dimensional conflict dimension, more specifically, a left–right dimension. If a policy view is part of the ideology of political parties, and particularly of the political elites, and not of the masses, elections will fail to communicate the view of the electorate on that issue. Therefore, political representation will fail, insofar as we see political representation as the mechanism 'by which political leaders act in accordance with the wants, needs and demands of the public in making government policy' (Luttbeg 1974: 3).

This argument concurs with the function that Downs attributes to ideologies. Downs's theory is based on the assumption that different ideologies can be ordered in a one-dimensional space; that is, these ideologies are part of the same conflict dimension. Downs assumes that political preferences can be ranked on a scale from left to right, where the left end of the scale represents full government control and the right end means a completely free market. In his view, ideologies are useful to parties as well as to voters: 'Voters do not know in great detail what the decisions of the government are, and cannot find out except at a significant cost. . . . Under these conditions, many a voter finds party ideologies useful because they remove the necessity of his relating every issue to his own philosophy. Ideologies help him focus attention on the differences between parties; therefore, they can be used as samples of all the differentiating stands. With this short cut a voter can save himself the cost of being informed upon a wider range of issues' (Downs 1957: 98).

Ideologies are equally useful for political parties: 'Each party realizes that some citizens vote by means of ideologies rather than policies; hence it fashions an ideology which it believes will attract the greatest number of votes' (Downs 1957: 100). In other words, political parties use ideology as a short cut in the same way as the voters do. Ideology helps parties avoid the necessity of relating each policy decision directly to voter reaction, thereby reducing the cost of decision-making (Downs 1957: 101–2).

In the delegate model of political representation, belief systems play a less obvious but equally important role. The intent to follow the will of the people is hardly effective if what people want is misunderstood (Holmberg 1989: 23). Therefore, the effectiveness of such a model of linkage depends first on the will to represent the people, and second, on the accuracy of the delegates' perception of the will of the people.

How do members of parliament assess the will of the people? Some cases are easier to assess than others. At first sight members of parliament in a district system do have an advantage. They can limit the estimate of their voters' sentiments to a well-defined geographical unit. However, as we have argued elsewhere (Thomassen 1994), salient political issues in a modern state more often than not cross-cut territorial boundaries and are—if anything— reflections of group interests rather than territorial conflicts. Under these circumstances I can only agree with Converse and Pierce (1986: 221) that 'the representative only rarely possesses an up-to-date direct measurement of his constituents' policy preferences'. Therefore, 'he must try to estimate the sentiments of his district from the bits and pieces of information that he has about his constituents. If, for example, he thinks of his district as leftist, he is likely to imagine that when an issue like the development of a nuclear strike force emerges on the political scene, sentiment in his constituency will be negative toward the idea.' Certainly in a party-dominated parliamentary system, the tendency of MPs to estimate the policy views of their (or their party's) voters on the basis of their party's ideological stand will be very strong. The accuracy of that estimate will not only depend on their ability to assess the ideological position of the voters, but also and equally important will be the extent to which the views of the electorate on that particular issue are constrained by a common ideology.

The major conclusion of the argument so far is that both models of linkage —the responsible party model and the delegate model—can be effective models of linkage only if the political elite and the mass public share a common belief system. Without such a common yardstick, effective political communication seems unlikely. Therefore, as Kinder puts it, 'the extraordinary interest in the possibility of ideological reasoning was and still is an expression of concern for the quality and very possibility of democratic forms of government' (Kinder 1983: 391).

Does such a common yardstick exist? The evidence with respect to this question seems to be confusing and contradictory. In his seminal article more than thirty years ago Converse (1964) gave a clear answer to this question: 'parallel to ignorance and confusion over these ideological dimensions among the less informed is a general decline in constraint among specific belief elements that such dimensions help to organize. It cannot therefore be claimed that the mass public shares ideological patterns of belief with relevant elites and at a specific level anymore than it shares the abstract conceptual frames of reference' (Converse 1964: 231). Converse measured the constraint among issues simply by calculating correlation coefficients between specific issue beliefs. The correlation coefficients, and therefore the constraints, among the mass public were dramatically lower than among the political elite (candidates for the 1958 US Congress). Moreover, Converse found that these low figures could not be accounted for by idiosyncratic belief systems but were mostly due to a lack of real attitudes among parts of the mass public. Therefore, a possible lack of congruence between the political elite and the mass public cannot be attributed to a difference of opinion between the two levels but is due to the fact that there is nothing to represent.

It has been argued before that Converse's verdict on the existence of belief systems among the mass public is not necessarily valid for all times and places. What was true in the somewhat apolitical 1950s in the USA is not necessarily true in the more polarized political situation of the 1960s and 1970s (for reviews of the relevant literature, see Kinder 1983 and Sniderman 1993). Also, what is true in the USA with its presidential system, where political parties are not much more than loose federations, is not necessarily true in the parliamentary systems of western Europe, where political parties still represent the ideological translation of the cleavage structure in society. In

Sweden, for instance, people appear to have attitudes that are more stable, more constrained, and more closely linked to voting behaviour than in the United States (Granberg and Holmberg 1988: 67 and 82). According to Granberg and Holmberg, 'Converse, together with his critics and supporters, may have tacitly and unintentionally led to an underestimation of what voters can be like and what they can do . . . the level of constraint, issue voting, and attitude stability that can be observed at the individual level may be presumed to vary as a direct function of the extent to which the people are living in a political system which has strong parties with well-known positions on an ideological dimension encompassing most contemporary issues on the political agenda' (Granberg and Holmberg 1988: 86).

There are among the many observers those who tend to believe that policy conflicts in Western societies are becoming one-dimensional, certainly in the countries of concern here (Fuchs and Klingemann 1989; Sani and Sartori 1983). There is a growing consensus that the left–right dimension is the main dimension of competition between political parties in west European countries. A similar role is attributed to the liberal–conservative dimension in the United States.

Moreover, the existing empirical evidence seems to demonstrate that not only the political elite but those in the mass public as well are able to think about political issues using the language of left and right. According to Fuchs and Klingemann (1989: 205) the left–right schema can function as a generalized mechanism for the reduction of complexity, which serves primarily to provide an orientation function for individuals and a communications function for the political system. In most countries people have remarkably little difficulty expressing their own policy positions in left–right terms. And, likewise, they generally are able to locate political parties along the same dimension.Therefore, the language of 'left' and 'right' seems to create a unidimensional discourse providing the common yardstick for masses and elites that is required in a model of political representation (Huber and Powell 1994: 293).

However, if all this is true, we are left with a puzzle. If the left–right dimension provides both the masses and the elites with the common yardstick we are looking for, and if there is such a high level of congruence between the two levels in terms of left–right self-identification, how can we then explain that most studies of representation reveal a high level of congruence between masses and elites on some issues, but a very low level on other issues? Repeatedly higher levels of congruence were found on issues related to the social class cleavage, like income and tax policy, than on issues related to the libertarian/traditional dimension, like foreign aid, immigration, and law and order (Dalton 1988; Thomassen 1976; Thomassen and Schmitt 1997).

SOLVING A PUZZLE

In the remainder of this chapter we shall try to solve this puzzle. The key to our argument is that the left–right dimension has gradually developed into the single relevant conflict dimension for which we are looking. Such a development could be interpreted in two different ways. Traditionally, the meaning of left and right is mainly associated with the class conflict. Accordingly, the first interpretation is that the left–right dimension is still nothing other than the political translation of the class cleavage; in this interpretation, this is the only significant conflict dimension left. Therefore, the political behaviour of both the mass public and the political elite is dictated by their position on this dimension. Sani and Sartori's distinction between a space of competition and a domain of identification seems to refer to a situation where different policy dimensions still exist, but where only the class cleavage retains its political significance (Sani and Sartori 1983: 330). The consequence for the process of political representation is that only on issues related to the traditional class cleavage is the left–right dimension an effective instrument of communication between mass and elite. However, from a democratic point of view this is of minor importance, because other issues have hardly any political salience.

A second interpretation is that the left–right dimension is such a powerful instrument of communication because it has gradually absorbed all other conflict dimensions and issues. Historically, in countries like the Netherlands and France, left versus right was even more associated with the religious–secular than with the class conflict. More recently it has been argued that the left–right dimension has absorbed the materialist-post-materialist and the libertarian-traditional contrasts, in addition to, or even instead of, the class conflict (Inglehart 1977; Kitschelt and Hellemans 1990; Knutsen 1995).

However, the extent to which this is the case remains a matter of empirical evidence. It would not be realistic to expect that among the mass public all kinds of issues are completely constrained by the left–right dimension. It is our contention that the extent to which this is the case will depend on the traditional relationship between an issue and the core of the left–right dimension. This core historically was and still is the class cleavage. The less related an issue is to this basic cleavage dimension, the higher the level of abstraction that is required to relate the issue to the core of the ideological framework. Because we can assume that the belief system of the political elite is more elaborate than that of the mass public, we can expect larger differences between structural and non-structural issues among the mass public than among the political elite.

From the argument so far, more expectations can be deduced. If the left–right dimension is the main instrument of communication between the masses and the elite, one can expect that political parties will stress their distinctive features in terms of this dimension and related issues. As a consequence voters will make their choice on the same basis. Therefore, it is to be expected that policy differences between parties and between the voters of different parties are most distinct on the left–right dimension and on issues directly related to that dimension. For the same reason party positions on the left–right dimension and related issues will be a more accurate reflection of the policy preferences of their voters. Also, in cases where politicians have no direct way of knowing voters' issue positions, they will deduce voters' positions from what is known about the more general position of the electorate on the left–right continuum (Converse and Pierce 1986: 653–5). However, the less related an issue is to the social class cleavage, the less reliable this left–right position is as a predictor of voters' policy views.

In summary, the following hypotheses can be deduced from the argument above:

Hypothesis I. The more an issue is related to the social class cleavage, the higher the correlation will be between that position and the left–right position.

Hypothesis II. The more related an issue is to the social class cleavage, the more distinct party differences will be, both at the mass and the elite levels.

Hypothesis 3. The more related an issue is to the social class cleavage, the higher the level of congruence between members of parliament and the voters of their party.

Hypothesis 4. The more related an issue is to the social class cleavage, the more accurate the perception of members of parliament of their voters' positions.

These hypotheses are tested against data from the Netherlands, Germany, Sweden, and the United States. Where appropriate, the results are compared with data reported on the French study by Converse and Pierce (Converse and Pierce 1986: ch. 7). The Dutch data are primarily from a study on political representation conducted in 1971–2. In this study both members of parliament and a sample from the electorate were asked to locate themselves on a left–right scale and on seven bipolar issue-scales. In addition members of parliament were asked where they would locate their voters on these scales, whereas the voters were asked to locate the seven major parties.[1] This study

---

[1] In the parliamentary study nine-point rating scales were used that could simply be transformed into the seven-point rating scales that were used in the voters study.

was repeated in 1977–9 and 1989–90. Where appropriate, data from these later studies are used as well; however, the data are less useful for our purposes because they contain fewer issues. The Swedish data are from the 1988 Swedish representation study comprising interviews with both members of the Riksdag and a sample of the electorate. The design of the German representation study from 1988–9 was quite similar, consisting of interviews with members of the Bundestag and a sample of the electorate. However, the format of the issue questions was different from that in the Dutch and the Swedish studies. That is, respondents were asked how important they considered each issue, rather than their position on a rating scale as in the Dutch and Swedish studies.

In the United States the elite data are not from members of the US Congress, but from a sample of the delegates to the Democratic and Republican conventions in 1988. The data on the electorate are from the National Election Study in 1988. Delegates were asked to rate their own position on a number of seven-point issue-scales, including the liberal–conservative domain. In addition they were asked to rate their perception of the position of a few other groups, including the national electorate of their party.

LEFT–RIGHT AND ISSUE POSITIONS

First, we need to decide to what extent different issue domains are related to the core of the left–right dimension. The traditional way to measure this is by computing the correlations between positions taken on issue scales and on a left–right scale. In this case this procedure would leave us with a pure tautology. Before we can test our hypotheses, we need to consider an independent assessment of the relationship of different policy domains to the core of the left–right dimension.

Issues that are related to the basic cleavages in a society can be called *structural issues*. The following structural issues are related to the class cleavage in society: nationalization, industrial democracy and participation democracy, income policy, social equality, taxes, and unemployment (Lane and Ersson 1987: 257). We shall abstain from any further differentiation within the remaining category of non-structural issues and from deciding whether they are theoretically related to the class cleavage. Not only would it be difficult to underpin such a differentiation theoretically, but also the number of issues available would make it close to impossible to test the hypotheses using such refined categories. Therefore, all hypotheses are tested using a simple dichotomy between structural and non-structural issues.

In the Dutch study three issues qualify as structural issues: income policy, workers' participation, and tax policy. In the Swedish case we consider the following as structural issues: reducing income differences, privatization of health care, reducing the size of the public sector, and a six-hour work day. In the German study, we consider the following structural issues: less competition and working pressure, more influence for trade unions, and work for everybody. In the American case none of the issues qualified as a structural issue in relation to the class cleavage. Therefore, the hypotheses cannot be tested against the American data. However, the US data are still useful for our analysis, for a different reason. Although all four hypotheses refer to the difference between structural and non-structural issues, we should also take possible system effects into consideration. American politics is often assumed to be less ideological and politicized than European politics, mainly because of the presidential system and the loose two-party system. Therefore, one should expect that issues in the USA are less constrained by a single ideological dimension and that parties are less distinct and coherent, which does not lead to the best conditions for a high consensus between party leaders and their rank and file or for an accurate perception by the political elite of their party followers.

The European countries included here can be expected to be different. All of them are parliamentary systems with well-disciplined parties, which are for the most part still rooted in the traditional cleavage system. It is hard to predict any differences between them. With their PR systems, Sweden and the Netherlands have a more extended party system than Germany, which might lead those countries to more distinct parties that are closer to their voters, because each party can represent a smaller segment of the electorate. This would also make it easier for politicians to know the opinions of their voters.

The essential data needed to test the four hypotheses are presented in Table 3.1, where the Roman numbers I to IV refer to the respective hypotheses. The correlations between the left–right dimension and different issues are presented in the first two columns. What is most striking in looking at these columns is the difference in the size of the correlations between masses and elites in all four countries, both on structural and non-structural issues. This difference confirms the well-known phenomenon that the constraints among the political elite are much higher than among the mass public. However, there is hardly any evidence in support of hypothesis I. Sweden is the only case in which the correlations for structural issues are at least higher than for non-structural issues, both among the mass public and members of parliament. Also, the difference between structural and non-structural issues is larger among the voters than among the MPs. This is what we would expect, because the political elite are more sophisticated than the mass public and therefore have a more elaborate belief system. In contrast to the mass

TABLE 3.1. The effects of structural vs non-structural issues

Issues	I L–R and issues[a] voters	MPs	II Party and issues[b] voters	MPs	III Difference[c] MPs/voters	IV Perception[d] MPs/voters	V Extension[e] Voters	MPs
The Netherlands								
Equality of incomes	−0.20	−0.65	0.14	0.62	11.09	4.86	32.5	64.5
Workers' participation	−0.26	−0.58	0.15	0.57	12.98	5.69	35.8	39.3
Tax policy	0.14	0.67	0.02	0.62	24.45	19.21	13.2	55.8
structural issues	**0.20**	**0.63**	**0.10**	**0.60**	**16.17**	**9.92**	**27.1**	**54.1**
Abortion	−0.32	−0.32	0.19	0.61	11.43	7.59	41.2	58.3
Law and order	0.24	0.74	0.05	0.51	18.38	10.74	22.3	41.7
Foreign aid	0.04	0.56	0.02	0.51	17.95	6.62	14.0	42.3
Defence policy	0.33	0.67	0.14	0.63	11.40	15.31	29.2	61.7
non-structural issues	**0.23**	**0.57**	**0.10**	**0.56**	**14.79**	**10.06**	**26.7**	**51.0**
Left–Right			0.35	0.67	20.17	10.69	43.3	49.5
Sweden								
Reduce public sector	−0.45	−0.80	0.26	0.78	13.60	20.00	54.5	93.0
Reduce income differences	0.37	0.68	0.17	0.57	8.75	20.30	40.2	56.7
Privatization health care	−0.47	−0.80	0.28	0.86	21.25	25.70	49.7	95.5
Six hours work day	0.34	0.63	0.17	0.51	13.25	19.04	43.7	81.0
structural issues	**0.41**	**0.73**	**0.22**	**0.68**	**14.21**	**21.26**	**47.0**	**81.5**
Reduce defence spending	0.28	0.69	0.13	0.63	15.12	27.00	45.5	77.2
Ban driving in inner cities	0.20	0.59	0.07	0.51	13.00	25.75	30.2	71.2
Allow TV-commercials	−0.25	−0.70	0.07	0.69	26.58	26.96	32.5	88.0
More day care centres	0.29	0.67	0.13	0.59	13.08	17.54	27.2	57.7
Retain nuclear power	−0.19	−0.59	0.16	0.62	19.87	24.04	43.7	91.0
EU-membership	−0.33	−0.67	0.16	0.69	25.87	33.12	51.0	87.2
non-structural issues	**0.26**	**0.65**	**0.12**	**0.62**	**18.92**	**25.73**	**38.3**	**78.7**
Left–right			0.53	0.74	7.33	3.43	51.5	65.6
Germany								
Less competitive spirit	−0.10	−0.48	0.02	0.29	19.50		7.25	46.0
More influence trade unions	−0.25	−0.56	0.11	0.47	11.19		21.7	42.0
Work for everybody	−0.06	−0.45	0.01	0.27	14.43		6.7	38.7
structural issues	**0.14**	**0.50**	**0.05**	**0.34**	**15.04**		**11.9**	**42.2**

TABLE 3.1. Cont'd

Issues	I L-R and issues[a] voters	MPs	II Party and issues[b] voters	MPs	III Difference[c] MPs/voters	IV Perception[d] MPs/voters	V Extension[e] Voters	MPs
Further progress	0.11	0.58	0.01	0.47	20.25		10.7	72.2
More citizen participation	-0.12	-0.51	0.03	0.29	12.56		10.2	45.2
Law and order	0.19	0.52	0.04	0.36	25.69		21.7	56.7
Limit right to demonstrate	0.29	0.46	0.07	0.25	28.50		32.5	30.5
Environment and nature	-0.09	-0.27	0.03	0.19	2.87		10.5	12.0
Making abortion easier	-0.18	-0.62	0.06	0.53	14.56		28.5	72.0
Influence citizens' initiatives	-0.12	-0.48	0.03	0.47	28.19		17.2	73.7
Use of nuclear power	0.22	0.74	0.06	0.70	21.25		30.7	78.5
non-structural issues	**0.16**	**0.52**	**0.04**	**0.40**	**19.23**		**20.2**	**55.1**
Left-right			0.35	0.55	9.72		30.7	36.3
United States								
Abortion	-0.16	-0.55	0.00	0.18	6.50	18.83	0.8	13.8
Defence spending	0.18	-0.72	0.07	0.41	23.75	7.25	13.5	34.0
Relations with Russia	0.12	0.57	0.00	0.22	12.83	9.50	4.5	26.2
Position of blacks	0.20	0.67	0.04	0.29	13.83	17.33	12.8	32.2
Womens' role	0.15	0.50	0.00	0.16	9.25	13.23	11.8	20.0
all issues	**0.16**	**0.60**	**0.02**	**0.25**	**13.23**	**10.50**	**6.7**	**25.2**
Liberal–Conservative			0.10	0.53	10.60		2.00	41.2

[a] Entries are Pearson correlation coefficients between left–right and issue self-placements.

[b] Entries are etas squared.

[c] Entries are weighed difference scores between MPs and voters according to the formula $\dfrac{\Sigma_p(A-B)}{P \times M} \times 100$

[d] Entries are weighed difference scores between MPs, perception of voters' positions and voters' self-placements. For calculation of scores, see n. c.

[e] Entries are the differences between the two most extreme parties according to the formula $\dfrac{X-Y}{M} \times 100$, where X = the most leftist party, Y = the most rightist party, M = the maximal difference.

where p = number of parties, A = mean score of MPs, B = mean score of voters, M = maximal difference.

public, the political elite more easily absorb non-structural issues within the same ideological domain as structural issues. However, there is no support for this argument in the Dutch and German data. Therefore, we can only conclude that there is insufficient and inconsistent support for hypothesis I.

PARTY AFFILIATION AND ISSUE POSITIONS

Hypothesis II suggests that at both the mass and elite levels, the more an issue is related to the social class cleavage, the more distinct party differences will be, and the more issue positions will be constrained by party affiliations. Appropriate data are available for Germany, the Netherlands, Sweden, and the United States, although we cannot make a distinction between structural and non-structural issues in the American case. To determine to what extent issue positions are constrained by party affiliation, we assess which part of the total variance of issue positions is due to differences *between* parties, compared with differences *within* parties. Of course, the classic statistical procedure to determine this is analysis of variance. Columns 3 and 4 of Table 3.1 present the squared etas for all issues in all countries at both levels. Also included are the average squared etas for structural versus non-structural issues.

These data are very informative with respect to the effectiveness of the responsible party model as a model of linkage. According to this model, as we observed above, political parties should be internally coherent and distinguish themselves from one another in order to offer a clear choice to the voters. The theoretical requirements of the model would be met perfectly if there were no *within-party* variance; that is, that all variance would be due to the differences *between* parties. This would result in an eta of 1.00.

In theory, voters vote for the party that is closest to their own policy preferences. Higher eta values indicate that the voters have managed to vote for the party representing their views, although these statistics say nothing, of course, about the causal sequence.

According to hypothesis II, we would expect structural issues to have higher etas for structural than non-structural issues, both among the political elite and the mass public. However, there is hardly any evidence in support of this hypothesis. Among Dutch and Swedish elites the differences are at least in the predicted direction, but the differences are rather small. The data from the electorate tell a similar story to that of hypothesis I: only the Swedish data are consistent with our expectations.

Although these data offer little evidence in support of the hypothesis, they still contain information that is most relevant for the general research question of this chapter. There is an impressive difference between political elites and masses to the extent that their views on specific policy issues are constrained by party affiliation. At least in the European countries this difference is much less in the case of the left–right dimension. In all three countries the etas squared for the elites are less than twice as high as that for the electorate. The most essential difference between masses and elites is the extent to which the etas tumble down among the electorate once we move to specific issues. Among the elites these etas are not much lower, and in some cases even higher, than for the left–right dimension. Except for two cases in Sweden (both structural issues) all values are below 0.20. What this apparently means is that the left–right dimension is in the abstract an effective instrument of political communication between masses and elites: it enables political parties to distinguish themselves, and it is strongly related to the party choice of the electorate. But whereas among the elite these party differences go together with comparable differences on specific issues, this is obviously not the case among the electorate. Therefore, in most cases the choice of a particular party says hardly anything about specific policy preferences. In the United States, as expected, the elites of the two major political parties are less distinct than their European counterparts, both on the liberal–conservative dimension and on specific issues. The policy views of the electorate are hardly constrained by party preference at all, reflecting a two-party system where parties are forced to behave according to a Downsian strategy; that is, to stay close to the median voter.

POLICY CONGRUENCE

Hypothesis III suggests that the level of policy congruence between masses and elites will depend on the issue. The level is expected to be higher for structural than for non-structural issues. We look at the extent to which the political elites reflect the policy views of the electorate at the level of the party system and at the level of individual parties.

From the perspective of the party system, it is relevant to what extent the spectrum of parties at the elite level reflects the spectrum at the mass level. Policy congruence, as measured by the issue scales, would be perfect if all parties were at exactly the same place at both levels. This implies that the *relative positions* of the parties, or the rank order of the parties, should be the same at both levels, and that the *extension* of the party system; that is, the distance between the two most extreme parties, should be equal (cf. Schmitt and Thomassen, forthcoming). One can get an impression of the extent to which the party system at the elite level reflects its counterpart at the electorate level by comparing the mean scores in Table 3.2. A measure of the extension of the party system is presented in the last two columns of Table 3.1.

Although hypothesis III does not refer to the left–right (or liberal–conservative) dimension itself, we have presented the scores on this dimension as well. They are the best indication we have of the 'true' position of both

TABLE 3.2. Mean issue positions of voters and political elites; perception of voters' position by the elite

(*a*) *The Netherlands*

	PvdA	D66	DS'70	ARP	KVP	CHU	VVD
Reduce income differences							
MPs	1.46	2.56	1.71	2.62	2.62	2.50	5.33
voters	2.16	2.45	2.65	3.44	2.93	3.06	4.11
perception	1.56	2.78	2.71	3.23	2.97	3.20	5.27
Workers' participation							
MPs	1.44	1.89	2.14	2.00	1.76	2.00	3.80
voters	1.96	2.32	2.82	3.15	3.18	2.94	4.11
perception	1.56	2.22	2.71	2.69	2.26	2.90	4.47
Tax policy							
MPs	1.77	2.67	5.43	3.38	2.74	3.40	5.12
voters	4.86	4.62	4.98	4.51	4.87	4.19	4.39
perception	2.64	2.89	6.00	4.08	3.62	4.20	5.80
Abortion							
MPs	1.82	1.44	1.83	3.77	4.94	3.60	1.88
voters	2.46	2.07	2.51	4.54	4.11	4.20	2.53
perception	2.05	1.80	3.14	5.15	5.15	4.40	2.56
Law and order							
MPs	2.56	2.90	5.00	4.23	4.24	4.70	5.06
voters	4.91	4.26	5.29	5.28	5.50	5.57	5.60
perception	3.85	2.80	5.71	5.08	4.71	5.20	5.81
Foreign aid							
MPs	1.77	2.00	4.43	2.58	2.69	2.80	4.31
voters	4.28	3.94	4.35	3.51	3.58	3.97	4.29
perception	3.56	3.09	4.86	3.50	3.66	4.00	4.87
Defence policy							
MPs	2.24	2.44	5.86	5.38	4.26	5.50	5.94
voters	3.14	3.05	4.35	4.80	4.27	4.46	4.80
perception	2.24	2.33	5.86	5.46	4.50	5.80	5.87
Left–Right							
MPs	1.90	2.50	3.00	3.69	3.40	4.00	4.87
voters	2.91	3.43	4.16	5.51	5.29	5.16	4.83
perception	2.46	2.90	3.71	4.92	3.97	4.55	5.37

(b) *Sweden*

	Comm	S-D	CP	LIB	CON	GREEN
Reduce income differences						
MPs	1.26	1.48	2.07	2.97	3.53	1.68
voters	1.62	2.11	2.38	2.79	3.23	1.98
perception	1.00	1.13	1.10	2.16	3.62	1.00
Reduce public sector						
MPs	4.84	4.42	2.93	1.85	1.12	3.10
voters	4.10	3.61	2.70	2.49	1.92	3.14
perception	5.00	4.92	2.44	1.57	1.00	2.65
Privatization health care						
MPs	5.00	4.54	2.57	1.33	1.18	3.21
voters	3.77	3.36	2.46	2.08	1.78	1.98
perception	5.00	4.68	1.95	1.00	1.00	3.25
Six-hour working day						
MPs	1.10	2.20	3.05	3.95	4.36	1.68
voters	1.71	2.13	2.95	2.91	3.46	2.14
perception	1.00	1.79	3.15	4.32	4.65	1.42
Reduce defence spending						
MPs	1.79	2.82	4.10	4.12	4.88	1.79
voters	2.25	3.17	3.61	3.51	4.07	2.70
perception	1.00	2.22	5.00	4.60	4.80	1.63
Ban driving in inner cities						
MPs	1.37	2.16	1.90	3.17	3.95	1.10
voters	1.94	2.38	2.19	2.76	2.99	1.78
perception	1.00	2.26	1.42	3.63	4.70	1.00
Allow commercial TV						
MPs	4.79	4.05	2.29	1.50	1.27	4.53
voters	3.14	2.56	2.61	2.13	1.84	2.81
perception	4.79	3.18	1.41	1.09	1.00	4.33
More day care centres						
MPs	1.06	1.24	2.43	1.76	3.37	2.44
voters	1.70	1.89	2.79	2.36	2.74	2.18
perception	1.00	1.00	2.30	1.49	3.57	1.75
Retain nuclear power						
MPs	4.95	4.08	4.95	3.20	1.36	5.00
voters	3.90	3.18	3.90	3.03	2.16	4.20
perception	4.79	4.26	4.90	3.87	1.00	5.00
EEC membership						
MPs	4.79	4.09	4.32	2.26	1.41	4.90
voters	3.57	2.86	2.79	2.20	1.79	3.11
perception	5.00	4.46	4.51	1.61	1.07	5.00
Left–Right						
MPs	1.32	3.10	5.07	5.48	7.88	4.24
voters	2.50	3.73	5.94	6.38	7.65	4.63
perception	2.00	4.01	5.63	6.00	7.79	5.12

(*c*) *Germany*

	CDU/CSU	SPD	FDP	GREENS
Less competitive spirit				
MPs	2.61	3.64	2.74	4.45
voters	3.83	4.09	3.86	4.12
More influence for Trade Unions				
MPs	1.88	3.56	1.90	3.23
voters	2.66	3.43	2.57	3.44
Work for everybody				
MPs	3.15	4.46	3.36	4.70
voters	4.35	4.50	4.27	4.54
Further progress				
MPs	4.43	3.38	4.25	1.54
voters	3.96	3.83	3.92	3.53
More citizen participation				
MPs	3.15	3.93	3.72	4.96
voters	3.90	4.16	4.10	4.31
Law and order				
MPs	3.44	2.33	2.57	1.17
voters	3.70	3.49	3.60	2.83
Limit right to demonstrate				
MPs	2.22	1.22	1.47	1.00
voters	3.12	2.57	2.96	1.82
Conservation environment				
MPs	4.35	4.79	4.53	4.83
voters	4.31	4.49	4.51	4.73
Making abortion easier				
MPs	1.17	3.07	2.48	4.05
voters	2.33	2.92	2.92	3.47
More influence for citizens initiatives				
MPs	1.57	2.27	1.76	4.52
voters	2.96	3.23	3.05	3.65
Use of nuclear power				
MPs	4.14	1.62	3.56	1.00
voters	3.07	2.60	3.05	1.84
Left–Right				
MPs	5.75	3.47	5.41	2.48
voters	6.61	4.47	5.68	3.85

(*d*) *United States*

	Democrates	Republicans
Abortion		
delegates	3.36	2.53
voters	2.81	2.76
perception		
Defence spending		
delegates	5.67	3.63
voters	3.56	4.37
perception	4.68	3.23
Relations with Russia		
delegates	5.67	3.81
voters	3.66	3.93
perception	2.96	4.10
Socio-economic position blacks		
delegates	2.86	4.79
voters	4.27	5.04
perception	3.36	4.81
Women's rights		
delegates	1.46	2.66
voters	2.56	2.67
perception	2.53	3.57
Liberal–Conservative		
delegates	2.91	5.38
voters	3.05	4.25
perception	3.38	5.08

elites and masses on the underlying dimension. The positions, or at least the rank order, of the parties on the left–right scale, both among masses and elites, are more or less consistent with the rank order that every knowledgeable observer of these polities would produce. The 'more or less' refers to two remarkable anomalies. First, the average score of the voters of the religious parties in the Netherlands was in 1971 clearly to the right of the VVD (Liberal Party). The MPs' position left of the VVD does more justice to the political programmes of these parties. The confusion is without any doubt due to the fact that for a part of the Christian population, the contrast between left and right still refers to the distinction between Christian and non-Christian.[2] The

---

[2] Later replications of this study indicate that this phenomenon is becoming part of history. In 1989, the average voter of the CDA (in which the three former Christian parties merged at the end of the 1970s) placed themselves more to the left than VVD voters did.

second anomaly is that in the Netherlands, all elite groups place themselves far more to the left than the voters do. This phenomenon is similar to that found by Converse and Pierce (1986: 128) in France. In Sweden one can see the same tendency but to less of an extent.[3] As a consequence, the mean difference (Table 3.1, column 5) between MPs and voters in the Netherlands on the left–right scale is larger than on all but one of the issues. In Germany the opposite is the case, whereas in Sweden the average distance is less than on any of the other issues.

In the three European countries the *extension* of the party system; that is, the weighted difference between the most left position and the most right position,[4] is hardly less at the mass level than at the elite level. In the United States, where the extension is less at both levels, the extension at the elite level is twice as much as that at the electoral level. In general, we can conclude that on the left–right scale party differences at the elite level pretty well reflect different party positions at the mass level. To what extent the left 'bias' of the elite has a substantive meaning, is not clear. The usual explanation for this phenomenon is the difference between mass culture and elite culture, which might account for part of the explanation, but not all of it. As we will see, political elites tend to place themselves far to the left of typical voters on issues that are related to the traditional libertarian dimension. It is quite possible that this tendency is reflected in the differences in self-placement on the left–right dimension.

According to hypothesis III, we should expect more congruence on structural than on non-structural issues. The data in Table 3.1 show immediately that there is little support for this hypothesis. Only in Sweden is the average extension on the structural issues clearly larger than on non-structural issues, at least among the electorate. On at least some of the non-structural issues, such as banning cars from inner cities, allowing commercials on TV, or the provision of more day care centres, the extension of the party spectrum at the elite level is larger than at the mass level. This has immediate consequences for the level of congruence as well. Small differences between parties at the

[3] In an earlier study, conducted in 1968–9 the effect was much stronger (Holmberg 1989: 19).

[4] The extension score was computed as the difference between the two most extreme parties, divided by the maximal difference (e.g. in the case of a 10-point scale this is 9), indicating the proportion of the maximal possible difference. This makes it possible to compare scores. However, one should be cautious in comparing the extension between countries. In the Netherlands only the seven larger parties were included. Including the small parties on the left and right side of the political spectrum undoubtedly would enlarge the extension.

mass level are tantamount to large discrepancies between mass and elite at the far wings of the party system. A clear example is the position of the Green party and the Communist parties on the issue of commercials on television. Whereas the MPs of both parties take an extreme position against commercials, their voters flock together in the middle of the scale.

In the Dutch case, we have distinguished three issues that are related to the class cleavage. Income policy and workers' participation meet the expectations to the extent that the mean scores of the MPs neatly reflect the positions of their voters, particularly when only the rank order of the parties is taken into account. Also, the extension at the mass level is hardly less than at the elite level. The tax issue does not meet the expectations at all. The issue was phrased as a choice between raising more taxes in order to have more money available for general welfare versus lowering taxes in order to enable everybody to spend their own money. At the mass level the message seems to be simple: nobody wants to pay taxes and everybody wants general welfare. At the elite level the parties' positions reflect their position on the left–right continuum.

The order of the parties on defence policy is consistent with the left–right order of parties, but the extension at the mass level is less than at the elite level. Law and order and aid to developing countries are issues on which the party differences at the elite level do not reflect the party differences at the mass level, where one can hardly speak of party differences. In the case of law and order, the rank order of parties is still more or less the same as that at the elite level, but the voters of all parties are far to the right; the consequence of this is that there is a large discrepancy between the voters and the MPs of the PvdA, the Dutch Labour Party. In the case of aid to developing countries, even the rank orders do not fit. Those of the religious parties, rather than the voters of the Labour party, take the most favourable position towards such aid, but the party differences are small and out of tune with the political elite.

The issue of abortion proves that it would be too simple to declare the Dutch party system a one-dimensional system. Party positions on this issue both at the mass and elite level reflect the religious cleavage, with all secular parties at one end of the scale and all religious parties on the other end. Therefore, the congruence between mass and elite on this issue is high, but the relative position of parties is perpendicular to the left–right distribution.

In Germany the discrepancy between mass and elite in terms of party differences is much larger than in the other countries. It is not unlikely that this discrepancy is due to a difference in question format rather than to differences between the political systems. German respondents were not asked to indicate their opinion on policy issues by placing themselves between two polar positions on an issue scale, but rather how important they considered different political problems. Although for many purposes the answers to these types of questions can be analysed in the same way as position issue scales, there seems to be a tendency among the mass public to consider these issues important, independent of their party preference. Therefore, the position of the voters on these scales tells us probably more about the mood of the country than about party differences at the mass level. As a consequence, the difference between mass and elite on these issues reveals which parties represent public opinion best. The position of the Greens on further economic progress and, to a lesser extent, the opinion of CDU/CSU and FDP representatives on the function of competition in society are examples of elite positions that are hardly reflected in the mass public. There is no evidence that the difference between structural and non-structural issues has any relationship at all with either the extension of the party spectrum or the level of congruence between voters and MPs. Among the issues with the largest extension, at both levels, are the issues of abortion and nuclear energy. As in the Dutch case abortion might be considered a structural issue, as long as we count the religious dimension as one of the traditional cleavage dimensions. However, from the perspective of this chapter, there is an important difference between the two countries. In Germany the rank order of parties, both at the mass and elite levels, is the same as that on the left–right dimension. Therefore, in terms of party competition, the left–right dimension has apparently absorbed the religious cleavage dimension.

In the United States the extension of the party spectrum at both levels is far less than that in the European countries. No doubt, this is mainly a function of the two-party system; the two parties are forced to the median position on the scale, or at least cannot allow themselves to take extreme positions.

Altogether, there is no unequivocal evidence to support hypothesis III. An interesting phenomenon is that the differences between mass and elite are consistent with the hypothesis on the left side of the political spectrum, but not on the right side. In general left parties are indeed representative of their voters on typical class issues such as income policy, but often not on non-material issues, such as law and order. What is revealed here is the old phenomenon of a left elite that is left not only in the socio-economic sense, but also in the *libertarian* sense, a combination that is less often found among the working class. At the same time parties on the right often represent policy views on socio-economic issues that are not even popular among their own voters, whereas their more traditional attitudes on non-material issues are shared by their rank and file.

ACCURACY OF ELITE PERCEPTIONS

Hypothesis IV is based on the assumption that in most cases members of parliament will try to simply estimate their voters' opinions on specific issues, not on the basis of knowing where their voters stand, but by projecting their own perception of the voters' left–right positions. Assuming that members can reasonably assess where their voters are on the left–right continuum, this strategy will be successful only when voters' issue positions are constrained by the left–right dimension. According to hypothesis I, this will be the case only for structural issues. Therefore, we can predict that MPs will more accurately perceive their voters' opinions regarding structural issues rather than non-structural issues. In principle relevant data are available for the Netherlands, Sweden, and the United States. However, for reasons mentioned above, hypothesis IV cannot be tested on the American data. Also, the perception questions used in Sweden followed a different format from that used for the questions on self-placement. Whereas both MPs and voters were asked to indicate their position on a full five-point scale, the perception question had only two categories, 1 and 5. As a consequence, the mean scores tend to be more extreme than might be expected in cases where a full five-point scale was used. As a result, the *extension* of the perceived position of the voters of different parties on the issue scales is larger than otherwise would have been the case. With the available information, there is no evidence of a systematic misperception of the voters' positions. Even though the question formats are not similar, one could still test hypothesis IV by comparing the differences for structural and non-structural issues. The average difference-score for non-structural issues is indeed larger than for structural issues (Table 3.1). On the basis of a similar study in 1985, Holmberg (1989: 24) could conclude that 'a clear pattern emerges proving that members did much better on old, highly politicized left–right issues than on newer, less politicized and non-left right issues'. This conclusion is a corroboration of hypothesis IV.

In the Netherlands MPs are to the left of their voters on many issues, and they are well aware of it. In particular within the PvdA, there is a clear pattern of MPs who are far to the left of their voters, yet who perceive correctly that their voters are more to the right. However, these MPs tend to underestimate the difference, which for a number of issues has led to their placing their voters between their own position and that of their true position. This is a general pattern, as one can see in Table 3.1. However, there is no support for hypothesis IV. Only three of the seven parties in Table 3.2 show a pattern that is consistent with the prediction that MPs will be better aware of their voters' opinions on structural issues.

CONCLUSION

In this chapter we have argued that the two major models of political representation—the responsible party model and the delegate model—can be effective as models of linkage only if the political elite and the mass public share a common one-dimensional belief system. Former research suggests that such a requirement is not totally unrealistic. Political cleavages in western societies have become more and more one-dimensional in the sense that the left–right dimension has gradually absorbed other conflict dimensions. Despite this evidence, we have maintained that it is hardly realistic to expect that all possible issues are constrained by a single dimension. We have argued that the correlation of issues with the left–right dimension will differ between policy domains. The more an issue is related to the traditional class cleavage, the more it is expected to be constrained by the left–right dimension. As a consequence, we had expected more policy congruence between mass and elites on class-related issues than on other issues. For that same reason we had predicted that the elites' perception of voters' policy views would be more accurate for class-related issues.

The results of our analysis are mixed. Essential for our argument is the not surprising finding that the differences in the level of constraint of issue positions between mass and elite are enormous. According to our main line of argument the lack of constraints of policy views at the mass level might lead to poor representation of the electorate's policy views of the electorate by the political elite. However, in general this is not what we found. Perhaps the most striking finding is the difference between the individual level and the aggregate level. Given the low levels of constraints, one would hardly expect a systematic relationship between party preference and issue positions at the mass level. Even though policy congruence between mass and elite is far from perfect, at least in Sweden and the United States the *order* of party positions at the aggregate level, is perfectly correlated to the left–right order of the parties for almost all issues both at the mass and elite level. In Germany the differences between parties at the mass level are too small to draw any valid conclusions. As mentioned above, these small differences are probably due to the question format. But even though the differences between the mean position of the voters of different parties are very small, the rank order of parties in most cases follows the left–right order. Therefore, at the aggregate level party systems do apparently represent differences in policy views among the electorate in a systematic way, despite the lack of constraints at the individual level.

One might even argue that ideological consistency among the elite that is not matched by the mass public might lead to serious misrepresentation. The most dramatic example of misrepresentation that we met is the case of law and order in the Netherlands. In the early seventies PvdA MPs took a position that was almost the opposite of their voters. This, as we have observed, is due to the fact that libertarianism is part of a left ideology among the elites, whereas this is not true among a large part of the mass public. As a consequence, MPs in this case lived in a different world from their voters. However, the voters got their revenge. Almost twenty years later a replication of this study proved that the situation had totally changed. The PvdA voters were on the average still where they were two decades before, but their representatives had moved to that position as well. It took the voters almost twenty years to close the gap, but they finally did, not because the ideological framework had changed, but because of the increasing salience of this particular issue that had been neglected by the political elite for such a long time (Thomassen and Zielonka 1992). What this single example proves is that models of political representation should be understood as models and nothing else. Each model of representation refers to a particular mechanism that might explain a possible congruence between mass and elite. But the real political world will never conform to just one of these mechanisms. Political representation is a dynamic process where several processes can lead to an agreement between the mass public and the elite. It is this mixture of political representation mechanisms in real life that makes the prospect of representative democracy less bleak than the evidence of the feasibility of each of the models separately might suggest.

APPENDIX: DUTCH REPRESENTATION STUDIES

The Dutch data used in this book originate from a series of representation studies performed in the years 1972, 1979, and 1990. Only the first study, in 1972, was designed as a mass/elite study. It includes a mass panel study (1970–1971–1972) and a study among all members of parliament (1972). The relevant mass data are in the 1971 study. Principal investigators of this first representation study were Philip Stouthard and Jacques Thomassen (Catholic University Tilburg), Hans Daalder (University of Leiden), and Warren Miller (University of Michigan). A book-length report (in Dutch) on this study is Thomassen 1976. The studies of 1979 and 1990 were not designed as a representation study in the sense that the study among members of parliament was not conducted in a direct relation with a mass study, but because the national election studies of 1977 and 1989 respectively replicated a number of issue questions from the Tilburg study, it was still possible to ask a limited number of issue questions that were comparable across levels and over time. The 1979 study was directed by Hans Daudt (university of Amsterdam), Rinus van Schendelen (Erasmus University Rotterdam), and Jacques Thomassen (University of Twente). Thomassen and van Schendelen also conducted the 1990 study in cooperation with Rudy Andeweg and Mei Lan Zielonka-Goei (University of Leiden). The major report on the 1979 study is Rinus van Schendelen, Jacques Thomassen, and Hans Daudt, *Leden van de Staten-Generaal*, 1981; on the 1990 study it is Jacques Thomassen, Rinus van Schendelen, and Mei Lan Zielonka, *De geachte afgevaardigde*, 1991. All studies among members of parliament are based on face-to-face interviews. The response rate in all these studies is high (more than 130 of a total of 150 members). All mass surveys are based on face-to-face interviews as well. They are well documented in English and available at the major data archives (the Dutch Steinmetz Archive, the ICPSR, and the Zentral Archiv in Cologne). The elite data were not deposited at the archives for reasons of data protection. Scholars interested in these data should get into contact with Jacquest Thomassen.

The following issues were included in one or more of the parliamentary (P) and mass surveys (M). The question format in all cases was a 7- or 9-point rating scale.

	P72	M71	P79	M81	P90	M89
1. abortion	X	X	X	X	X	X
2. law and order	X	X	X		X	
3. income policy	X	X	X	X	X	X
4. aid to developing countries	X	X	X	X		
5. co-determination of workers	X	X	X	X		
6. tax policy	X	X	X	X		
7. armed forces	X	X				
8. euthanasia					X	X
9. left–right	X	X	X	X	X	X

REFERENCES

Converse, Philip E. (1964), 'The Nature of Belief Systems in Mass Publics', in David E. Apter (ed.), *Ideology and Discontent* (New York: Free Press).
—— and Roy Pierce (1986), *Political Representation in France* (Cambridge, Mass.: Harvard University Press).
Dalton, Russell J. (1988), *Citizen Politics in Western Democracies* (Chatham: Chatham House Publishers).
Downs, Anthony (1957), *An Economic Theory of Democracy* (New York: Harper & Row).
Fuchs, Dieter, and Klingemann, Hans-Dieter (1989), 'The Left–Right Schema', in M. Kent Jennings, Jan W. van Deth, et al., *Continuities in Political Action: A Longitudinal Study of Political Orientations in Three Westerns Democracies* (Berlin: Walter de Gruyter).

Granberg, Donald, and Holmberg, Sören (1988), *The Political System Matters: Social Psychology and Voting Behavior in Sweden and the United States* (Cambridge, Mass.: Cambridge University Press).

Holmberg, Sören (1989), 'Political Representation in Sweden', *Scandinavian Political Studies*, 12: 1–35.

Huber, John D., and Powell, G. Bingham jr. (1994), 'Congruence between Citizens and Policymakers in two Versions of Liberal Democracy', *World Politics*, 46: 291–326.

Inglehart, Ronald (1977), *The Silent Revolution, Changing Values and Political Styles among Western Publics* (Princeton: Princeton University Press).

Kinder, Donald R. (1983), 'Diversity and Complexity in American Public Opinion', in Ada W. Finifter (ed.), *Political Science: The State of the Discipline* (Washington: The American Political Science Association).

Kitschelt, Herbert, and Hellemans, Staf (1990), 'The Left–Right Semantics and the New Politics Cleavage', *Comparative Political Studies*, 23: 210–38.

Klingemann, Hans-Dieter (1995), 'The Congruence of Party Positions and Voter Orientations: Left–Right Party Positions and Left–Right Voter Orientations in Western Europe', in Hans-Dieter Klingemann and Dieter Fuchs (eds.), *Citizens and the State* (Oxford: Oxford University Press).

Knutsen, Oddbjorn (1995), 'Value Orientations, Political Conflicts and Left–Right Identification: A Comparative Study', *European Journal for Political Research*, 28: 63–93.

Lane, Jan-Erik, and Ersson, Svante O. (1987), *Politics and Society in Western Europe* (London: Sage).

Luttbeg, Norman, R. (ed.) (1974), *Public Opinion and Public Policy: Models of Political Linkage*, 3rd edn. (Ithaca, NY: F. E. Peacock).

Miller, Warren E., and Stokes, Donald E. (1963), 'Constituency Influence in Congress', *American Political Science Review*, 57: 45–56.

Sani, Giacomo, and Sartori, Giovanni (1983), 'Polarization, Fragmentation and Competition in Western Democracies', in Hans Daalder and Peter Mair (eds.), *Western European Party Systems: Continuity and Change* (London: Sage).

Schmitt, Hermann, and Thomassen, Jacques (eds.) (1999), *Political Representation and Legitimacy in the European Union* (Oxford: Oxford University Press).

—— (forthcoming), 'Political Representation in the European Union: The Role of Political Parties', in Richard Gunther, Juan J. Linz, and José Ramon Montero (eds.), *Political Parties: Changing Roles in Contemporary Democracies*.

Sniderman, Paul M. (1993), 'The New Look in Public Opinion Research', in Ada W. Finifter (ed.), *Political Science: The State of the Discipline II* (Washington: American Political Science Association).

Thomassen, Jacques J. A. (1976), *Kiezers en gekozenen in een representatieve demokratie* (Alphen aan den Rijn: Samsom).

—— (1994), 'Empirical Research into Political Representation: Failing Democracy or Failing Models', in M. Kent Jennings and Thomas E. Mann (eds.), *Elections at Home and Abroad: Essays in Honor of Warren E. Miller* (Ann Arbor: University of Michigan Press).

—— and Jennings, M. Kent (1989), *Party Systems and Democracy*. Paper presented at the annual workshop of the workgroup on elections and parties, committee on political sociology, IPSA/ISA, Paris, 10–12 Apr. 1989.

—— and Schmitt, Hermann (1997), 'Political Representation in the European Union: Policy Congruence', *European Journal for Political Research*. 32/2: 165–84.

—— and Zielonka, Mei-Lan (1992), 'Het Parlement als Volksvertegenwoordiging', in J. J. A. Thomassen, M. P. C. M. van Schendelen, and M. L. Zielonka-Goei (eds.), *De geachte afgevaardigde . . . hoe kamerleden denken over het Nederlandse parlement* (Muidenberg: Coutinho).

4

The Language of Politics

A Study of Elite and Mass Understandings of Ideological Terminology in the United States and the Netherlands

Richard Herrera

The study of mass–elite relationships in this volume is pursued from a variety of approaches and through the use of a unique combination of survey data. While we are all interested in these linkages, this chapter takes a different look at those couplings by examining the nature of political discourse between the mass public and their representatives. Rather than focus on the positions held by mass and elite on a variety of political issues, this chapter inspects the abilities of the public and the political elite in the United States and the Netherlands to communicate with each other using a shared understanding of political language. To the extent that open and well-understood communication between mass and elite facilitates political representation, this contribution might be seen as a first step in the study of mass-elite communication patterns.

I start with the assumption that a common political language is a necessary condition for meaningful communication and certainly for properly functioning citizen–elite relationships. The development of politically meaningful public opinion, on which representative government rests, is essential to the vitality of that relationship. McClosky and Zaller (1984: 12) take this notion further arguing that the social and political learning that takes place among the mass citizenry 'requires that [they] be able to comprehend in some measure what is implicit in sophisticated political and economic discourse'.

The degree to which elites are able to communicate with the mass citizenry is of utmost importance to political schooling for the mass public. If one presumes that 'mass opinion is not self-generating [but] a response to the cues, proposals, and the visions propagated by the political activists', and 'is the product of an interaction between political influential and the mass of the people' (Key 1961: 557) then the quality of mass–elite linkages should be reflected in the degree to which there is a shared understanding of the meanings of the terms used to conduct some of the interaction.[1] Insofar as the tie between the public and the political elite is compromised by a failure to communicate political ideas, the ability of leaders to lead, and the mass public to respond to that leadership is hindered. Ultimately, the lack of mutually accepted articulation of opinion between elites and masses might well lead to 'the decay of democracies' (Key 1961: 558).

THE LEFT–RIGHT SCHEMA AND POLITICAL REPRESENTATION

One way in which the representation of mass views is facilitated is a shared language of politics. When elites and masses are speaking the same language we can expect views to be shared on political issues. As Miller and Levitin (1976: 173) point out,

Public response to political leadership is not instantaneous. Although there is inadequate critical evidence with which to test the point, the speed of mass response may well be, in part, a function of how quickly citizens comprehend, accept, and utilize the same political language, language such as 'liberal,' 'conservative,' 'right,' or 'left' that is used by political leaders and by the political elite.

Political leaders send messages to the public constantly. These messages take place in electronic, print, and personal forms of communication. While these messages appear in a variety of media, there are certain central concepts and terms that can be found in all of them. Political discourse in America and Europe often employs the left–right schema (Fuchs and Klingemann 1989). The terms 'leftist', 'rightist', 'liberal', and 'conservative' are common parlance in most representative democracies (Fuchs and Klingemann 1989: 203). In the United States, for example, some of the more critical terms for today's political world are 'liberal' and 'conservative' (Kerlinger 1984: 13). As Miller and Levitin (1976: 173) state, the words liberal and conservative are 'among the most frequently used words of the [American] political lexicon'. In Europe, the Netherlands in particular, leftist and rightist tend to be the terminology used to describe political ideology (Fuchs and Klingemann 1989).

---

[1] See also Page and Shapiro (1992) and Zaller (1992) for discussions of elite leadership of mass opinion and Zaller (1992: 268–74) for an elaboration on the direction of communication from elite to mass.

These ideological terms are used to describe a host of political issues and party platforms as well as candidates. For example, rather than describe in detail the stands taken by members of the US Congress on particular issues, those positions may be summarized with a 'liberalism/conservatism' score (Smith et al. 1990; Herrera et al. 1995). In addition to providing the parameters within which politics are discussed and debated, the meaning of these terms may provide the basis for a system of organized political thought, or belief system (Converse 1964: 207–14). Hence, scholars of public opinion emphasize the importance of a shared understanding of ideological terms by the mass public and the political elite regardless of the differences in the political sophistication the of elites and masses.

We know that the elites are better informed than the masses about politics. Political elites are also more sophisticated politically than the average voter. But one cannot assume that a gap in the levels of information means that the public is unable to understand the terminology of the elites. Nor do we know just how much political astuteness is required to achieve a rudimentary understanding of political communication. To the extent that a commonality of language is a prerequisite to an electorate attuned to politics and political debate, it is important to examine this first link in the political learning process of the citizenry. This study is designed to explore the ways in which citizens from similar political systems—representative democracies —yet quite different political cultures use political language and whether the mass and elite segments of those societies share similar understandings of those terms.

BACKGROUND

Studies of the recognition and understanding of the terminology of political ideology by the mass public began with Converse's (1964) landmark study. Though concerned with broader issues of the belief systems of the mass public, Converse's work also set in motion the impetus for analysis of the terms used to describe political ideology. More recent studies of ideological terminology in the United States (Conover et al. 1981; Knight 1990; Herrera 1996) have utilized new items in survey questionnaires that reference the ideological terms themselves as the referent to be defined by the respondent.[2] These studies have charted the ways in which the American public understands

---

[2] Converse (1964) used answers to open-ended questions that reference political parties. Beginning in 1978 the ANES began using open-ended questions that asked about the meanings of ideological terms separate from political parties.

the terms of political debate and, for the most part, have found remarkable stability in those attitudes from the mid-1970s through the late 1980s (Knight 1990; Herrera 1996).

The ways in which the mass public from the United States and European countries understand the left–right schema have been amply studied by Klingemann (1979a, 1979b, 1979c) and Fuchs and Klingemann (1989).[3] Klingemann, in his contributions to *Political Action*, provides a full account of how various levels of conceptualization affect the mass publics' understandings of the core terms of political discourse in the United States, Germany, the Netherlands, Britain, and Austria (1979a, 1979b, 1979c). In the sequel to the first volume, Fuchs and Klingemann (1994) revisit the recognition and understandings of the left–right schema by the mass citizenry in Germany, the Netherlands, and the United States. These studies are instructive and provide the theoretical and empirical bases for this inquiry.

The research elaborates upon earlier American and cross-national studies in important ways. First, I provide an update of mass understandings of ideological terms in both the United States and the Netherlands. The data used for the last examination of the American case were from 1988 (Herrera 1996) and the *Political Action* study's 1974 surveys were followed by subsequent ones in 1981 (Jennings and van Deth et al. 1989). Second, I employ survey data that, unlike the *Political Action* surveys, reference the ideological labels specific to the countries being studied—liberal/conservative in the United States and leftist/rightist in the Netherlands. Though the sets of ideological labels are functional equivalents (Fuchs and Klingemann 1989: 203), using these data allow us to rule out the effects of the referent when making comparisons. Finally, and most importantly, I incorporated data about the views of the political elite from the United States and the Netherlands in order to make comparisons with the beliefs held by the mass public. This study, then, represents the first cross-national examination of mass understandings of left–right terminology in the 1990s and the first ever to use elite surveys for mass–elite comparisons.

EXPECTATIONS

Though the use of ideological terminology is common and the labels likely to be readily understood, they are also terms that 'are uneasy and fraught with

---

[3] In the 1974 and 1981 *Political Action* surveys used by Klingemann (1979a, 1979b, 1979c) and Fuchs and Klingemann (1989), open-ended items about the meaning of ideological terms followed respondents' self-placement on a scale where left and right were the opposite choices.

the possibility of misunderstanding, simplification, and specific demands and appeals' (Jennings 1993: 440). McClosky and Zaller (1984: 189) elaborate on those sentiments stating that ideological terms 'arouse passionate feelings of support and opposition, so that universal agreement about their meaning is difficult to achieve'. Hence our expectations about shared understandings of political language by elite and mass should be limited.

Given much literature on mass–elite linkages (Converse 1964; Prothro and Grigg 1960; McClosky et al. 1960; McClosky 1964; McClosky and Zaller 1984; Miller 1988; Herrera et al. 1992), as well as on mass understandings of ideological terms (Klingemann 1979*a*, 1979*b*, 1979*c*; Conover et al. 1981; Fuchs and Klingemann 1989; Knight 1990; Herrera 1996) the expectations for the present discussion are simple. The extent of agreement between elites and masses on the understanding of the traditional terms of political debate will be modest, but will increase with the degree of political engagement of strata within the mass public (McClosky and Zaller 1984: 11). On the one hand, 'the liberal–conservative continuum is a rather high-order abstraction, and such abstractions are not typical analytical tools for the "man in the street"' (Converse 1964: 215). That said, of the many versions of mass–elite differences, 'persistent and varied participation is most heavily concentrated among the most sophisticated people' (Converse 1964: 226), suggesting that as one becomes more engaged politically, one will utilize more complex analytical tools. Hence, the expectation is that terms such as 'liberal' and 'conservative' in the United States and 'leftist' and 'rightist' in the Netherlands, may become common parlance with high levels of citizen participation. The ability to understand those terms in the same abstract form that is their nature should increase as well.

DATA

To proceed with an analysis of these matters it is necessary to identify populations and substrata of the mass public and representations of the political elite. More importantly, data that include items that directly reflect meanings attached to ideological terminology are called for. In a study of the commonality of political language, open-ended items that allow respondents to express their interpretations of abstractions without constraint, and that allow the researcher to directly assess notions of ideology, should be sought.

In the United States, the opportunity for direct measurement presents itself with data from the 1992 Convention Delegate Study (CDS) and the 1992 American National Election Study (ANES). The 1992 CDS was the fifth in a series of surveys of delegates to the Democratic and Republican national party conventions that began in 1972. In both the party delegate survey and the survey of the mass public open-ended questions about the meaning of ideological labels were posed in precisely the same format.

The questions put to both the mass public and national party delegates were:

People have different things in mind when they say that someone's political views are liberal or conservative. We'd like to know more about this. Let's start with liberal. What sorts of things do you have in mind when you say someone's political views are liberal?

And, what do you have in mind when you say that someone's political views are conservative?

The data from the Netherlands came from two studies, conducted four years apart, that posed questions to members of parliament and the mass public about their understandings of the terms 'leftist' and 'rightist'. The following questions were posed:

'Could you indicate what "leftist" means to you?'
'Could you also indicate what "rightist" means to you?'

The survey of members of the Dutch parliament, conducted in 1990, was the fourth in a series that began in 1968. The data from the mass public come from the 1994 Dutch National Election Study.

Though there is a four-year gap between the two Dutch studies, both practical and theoretical considerations persuade me none the less to incorporate the studies in the analysis. On the practical side, data of this sort—open-ended questions about the understandings of the core terms of political debate— are rare enough to obtain and corresponding surveys from the national elite are rarer still. The greater error would be to ignore the availability of these data rather than use them with appropriate caution. On the theoretical side, the attitudes of political elites on matters as fundamental as the meaning attached to ideological terms should be quite stable. Indeed, evidence in the American case suggests that we should be confident in the stability of attitudes held by elites (Herrera et al. 1995). In addition, among the Dutch mass public, studies of materialist and post-materialist values have shown high levels of stability (Inglehart 1989: 81–6; van Deth 1983) especially among those most engaged in politics (van Deth 1983). The same should therefore hold true for political elites in their understandings of ideological language. Hence, I am confident using these data.

For all four data sets, responses to the open-ended items were coded using the same scheme as used in categorizing responses in the American National Election Studies. The original coding schemes were then reorganized to produce six categories of answers: those that utilized general philosophy, group references, economic policy, specific domestic policy, foreign policy, and candidate and/or party references.[4] The general philosophy category includes descriptions such as 'accepting of change/favouring the status quo', 'advocating social welfare programmes/pro-free enterprise', 'socialism', and 'communism'. The group references category is used for descriptions of the concepts by groups associated with the labels. For example, descriptions of conservative as supporting 'big business' would warrant the identification of those responses as group references. The economic policy responses are 'spend–save' type of descriptions of the ideological labels. The domestic policy responses are those that dealt with specific issues such as favouring or opposing health insurance or nuclear power. Likewise, responses considered to be in the foreign policy category are those that described the terms war and peace or isolationism and internationalism. Finally, respondents who associated the labels with specific political parties or politicians had their response labelled as a candidate or party reference response. Only the first response coded was used in the analysis presented here.

There are, of course, a variety of ways in which the data might be coded to account for the variation in each country. The decision was made to use the American National Election Studies master code categories to ease the presentation of results. These categories, however, do not differ markedly from those used in other cross-national studies of the understandings of the left–right schema in which data from the Netherlands were included (Fuchs and Klingemann 1989: 212–15). In only one case do the categories not capture most of the responses to the items.[5] The only other difficulty may be in the crudeness of the most abstract category. Specifically, the general philosophy category may be too gross a classification, hiding important aspects of the meanings attached to the labels by both mass and elite. Therefore, additional analysis, using more refined groupings within the general philosophy category are also included.

THE VIEWS OF THE MASS PUBLIC

The first step in this analysis is to document what the public thinks about the ideological labels. Doing so provides the backdrop to the comparison between the public and elites.

The initial inspection of the overall distributions of responses reveals a mass public that responds to the ideological terms largely by reference to general

---

[4] These categories are the standard ANES master code categories.
[5] In the Dutch case, just under 10 per cent of respondents used 'affective' references to describe leftist and rightist, identifying the terms with 'good' or 'bad' people.

TABLE 4.1. Aggregate salience of meanings of ideological labels 1992 US mass sample

Category of response	Meaning of 'liberal'		Meaning of 'conservative'	
	Mass (%) (1)	Mass responding (%) (2)	Mass (%) (3)	Mass responding (%) (4)
General philosophy	35	62	36	63
Group references	3	5	4	7
Economic policy	7	12	10	17
Domestic policy	9	17	5	8
Foreign policy	—	1	1	3
Cand/party figure	2	3	2	3
Percentage not responding	44		42	
N	2,487	1,385	2,487	1,442

Note: Entries are the percentage of respondents whose answers fell into that category.
Source: 1992 American National Election Study.

TABLE 4.2. Aggregate salience of meanings of ideological labels, 1994 Dutch mass sample

Category of response	Meaning of 'leftist'		Meaning of 'rightist'	
	Mass (%) (1)	Mass responding (%) (2)	Mass (%) (3)	Mass responding (%) (4)
General philosophy	46	79	39	77
Group references	8	13	7	14
Economic policy	2	3	2	4
Domestic policy	1	2	1	1
Foreign policy	—	—	—	—
Cand/party figure	2	3	2	4
Percentage not responding	41		50	
N	1,812	1,063	1,812	912

Note: Entries are the percentage of respondents whose answers fell into that category.
Source: 1994 Dutch National Election Study.

philosophic themes. Pluralities of both the American and Dutch mass public made responses falling into that category (see columns 1 and 3 of Tables 4.1 and 4.2).[6] The frequencies in most of the other five categories are

---

[6] The term aggregate salience refers to the proportion of a given set of respondents who cite a given description of their understanding of the ideological terms (Kelley 1983: 61).

relatively small although, in the American case, substantial minorities make reference to the economic and domestic policy areas. Specifically, respondents more often use domestic policy referents to define liberal (9 per cent) but use them much less often to define conservative (5 per cent), preferring economic policy terms to describe instead (10 per cent). In the Dutch case the only other significant responses were references to groups associated with the ideological terms (8 per cent for leftist, 7 per cent for rightist).

Although the American and Dutch citizenry do not appear altogether ignorant of the meanings of ideological terms, they are none the less notable for their frequent inability to give any answer at all—a pattern to which we will return later.[7] Over 40 per cent of both samples did not offer any definitions of the labels; although both terms seem equally well understood. When the base for analysis is changed to include only those who responded to each item, the general pattern, of course, remains the same; for example, the proportions of responses falling into the general philosophy category rises to over 60 per cent and lesser usages increase proportionately (see columns 2 and 4 in Tables 4.1 and 4.2).[8]

Looking at the entire sample of respondents may cover up patterns within important subgroups. To explore this possibility, I stratified the data in two ways: to examine (1) how the politically active compare to the inactive, and (2) how self-identified ideologues view the ideological labels.[9]

As Table 4.3 illustrates, in the American case there are marked differences between voters and non-voters. The most obvious difference between the two groups of citizens is in the propensity to answer. More than twice as many non-voters as voters did not answer the questions. However, the apparent stark differences between voters and non-voters in frequency of category response evaporate once we examine only those who make some response.

---

[7] For both samples, 'don't know', 'no answer', and 'normative' responses were coded as not responding. The last type of response is an affective answer such as identifying the term with 'bad' or 'good' people. Including these responses in the Dutch case changes the percentage not responding by about 9 per cent. The change is smaller in the American sample.

[8] The general philosophy category was broken down further so that a more refined look at patterns of response may be made. Within the general philosophy category, three-quarters of respondents, both mass and elite, described conservative and liberal with the following categories: accepting of change/favouring the status quo; advocacy of social welfare programmes/pro-free enterprise; compassionate toward/uncaring of others; promoting individual reliance on/independence from government. See Tables 4.A and 4.B in the Appendix for general analyses based on these categories and the 'The Views of the Political Elite and the Mass Public' section for a discussion utilizing these categories in Tables 4.7*b*, 4.8*b*, 4.9*b* and 4.10*b*.

[9] In the American case, I differentiated between voters and non-voters, while in the Dutch analysis I used levels of interest in politics.

TABLE 4.3. Aggregate salience of meanings of ideological labels, 1992 US mass voters and non-voters

Category of response	Meaning of 'liberal'		Meaning of 'conservative'	
	Voters (%)	Non-voters (%)	Voters (%)	Non-voters (%)
General philosophy	61	69	63	61
Group references	6	2	7	6
Economic policy	13	7	17	20
Domestic policy	17	15	8	6
Foreign policy	1	1	1	1
Cand/party figure	3	5	3	3
Percentage not responding	30	74	29	70
N	1,179	202	1,203	235

Note: Entries are the percentage of respondents whose answers fell into that category. Figures are the percentage of only those responding to the items as are the base numbers of cases.

Source: 1992 American National Election Study.

Among those citizens who do offer definitions of terms there is little difference in voter and non-voter use of abstract philosophic references. In both cases, the percentage of respondents giving general, rather abstract philosophical answers is approximately 60 per cent. Beyond this, about the only insight added by comparing responses among voters and non-voters concerns the differential use of domestic and economic policy descriptors to describe the two terms, liberal and conservative. Both voters and non-voters make much use of domestic policy responses to define liberal while using economic policy terms to define conservative. Non-voters do not, however, use economic policy to describe liberal as frequently as do voters. Though the wide gulf in the proportions not responding at all to the general terms suggests caution, at this juncture it appears that among those Americans choosing not to go to the polls, persons who do offer a meaning or definition for the two abstractions share a common understanding of political terminology with those electorally active. Table 4.4 illustrates the breakdowns for the Dutch citizenry.

As was true for Americans, for the Dutch electorate, the largest differences between those interested in politics and those who are not is in the propensity to answer. There are step function decreases in the percentage of respondents offering a definition of the labels as we move from those most interested to those least interested in politics. Once we examine the responses of those who do answer the questions, we find few differences between citizens with varying degrees of interest in politics and their understandings of

TABLE 4.4. Aggregate salience of meanings of ideological labels, 1994 Dutch mass samples by level of interest in politics

Category of response	Meaning of 'leftist'			Meaning of 'rightist'		
	Very interested in politics (%)	Somewhat interested in politics (%)	Not interested in politics (%)	Very interested in politics (%)	Somewhat interested in politics (%)	Not interested in politics (%)
General philosophy	70	61	34	56	51	34
Group references	11	10	7	10	10	5
Economic policy	2	2	1	3	3	1
Domestic policy	1	2	2	1	2	2
Foreign policy	—	—	—	—	—	—
Cand/party figure	1	3	3	4	1	3
Percentage not responding	15	23	53	26	34	56
N	208	997	262	204	981	265

Note: Entries are the percentage of respondents whose answers fell into that category. Figures are the percentage of only those responding to the items as are the base numbers of cases.

Source: 1994 Dutch National Election Study.

political terminology. Most of the responses from all three groups fall into the general philosophy category, with moderate reductions in the propensity to use that type of response as interest in politics declines. In addition, the Dutch associate rightist and leftist with groups, in contrast with their American counterparts.

For both countries, then, level of activity and interest in politics seems to play a small role in differentiating the understandings of citizens with the discourse of politics. Although those not engaged in politics may make no use of the terms, those who do recognize the labels make similar associations regardless of their political activity.

IDEOLOGUES' VIEWS OF IDEOLOGICAL LABELS

The comparisons between self-described liberals, conservatives, leftists, and rightists anticipates the ultimate interest in comparisons between mass and elite. The basic goal is to see whether interpretations of our political terms are such that inter-group communication seems possible for very different groups among whom communication is needed to sustain political dialogue. Just as we are concerned with the ability of the political elite to communicate with the mass public, so too are we interested in the terms with which these groups in that mass public can talk to or about each other. In other words, can ideologues in the general population communicate or do they talk past each other? Tables 4.5 and 4.6 present the understanding of the terms liberal, conservative, leftist, and rightist for members of the mass public who differ on ideological self-identification.[10]

Among the ideologically engaged, self-proclaimed liberals, conservatives, leftists, and rightists among the mass public apparently think about the ideological terms in very similar ways. First, and foremost, both these groups tend to use general philosophical definitions in a majority of their responses. Consistent with our earlier analysis (Tables 4.1–4.4), for liberals, conservatives, leftists, and rightists the aggregate salience for two of the remaining five categories of response is very small (foreign policy and party or candidate references). Moreover, for the Dutch, only the general philosophy and group reference categories were relevant for leftists and rightists.

[10] In this analysis, liberals are those who placed themselves as extremely liberal, liberal, or slightly liberal and conservatives are those who chose extremely conservative, conservative, or slightly conservative to describe themselves. Leftists are those who identify themselves as extreme leftist or leaning in that direction while rightists placed themselves on the extreme right or lean toward the right. The analysis that follows utilizes only those who answered the items.

TABLE 4.5. Aggregate salience of meanings of ideological counterparts, 1992 US mass sample

Category of response	Meaning of 'liberal'		Meaning of 'conservative'	
	Liberals (%)	Conservatives (%)	Liberals (%)	Conservatives (%)
General philosophy	66	57	68	62
Group references	8	4	11	4
Economic policy	7	14	9	18
Domestic policy	16	20	8	10
Foreign policy	1	1	1	2
Cand/party figure	3	4	3	4
Percentage not responding	30	32	30	31
N	351	509	354	520

Note: Entries are the percentage of respondents answering whose answers fell into that category. Figures are the percentage of only those responding to the items as are the base numbers of cases.

Source: 1992 American National Election Study.

TABLE 4.6. Aggregate salience of meanings of ideological counterparts, 1994 Dutch mass sample

Category of response	Meaning of 'leftist'		Meaning of 'rightists'	
	Leftists (%)	Rightists (%)	Leftists (%)	Rightists (%)
General philosophy	67	54	50	52
Group references	12	8	10	9
Economic policy	2	2	3	3
Domestic policy	1	2	1	1
Foreign policy	—	—	—	—
Cand/party figure	2	4	3	2
Percentage not responding	28	30	29	30
N	692	683	692	669

Note: Entries are the percentage of respondents whose answers fell into that category. Figures are the percentage of only those responding to the items as are the base numbers of cases.

Source: 1994 Dutch National Election Study.

Among liberals and conservatives in the United States, both agree that 'liberal' is defined by domestic policy more than is 'conservative'. However, despite the common usage on four of six categories of response, liberals and conservatives disagree in two different associations with the terms liberal and conservative. The main difference between the two groups appears in the use of group attachments and economic policies to define the ideological terms. Liberals are more likely than conservatives to use group references in defining the abstract labels while conservatives are more likely to see the abstractions in terms of economic policy.[11]

SUMMARY

The American and Dutch mass publics show a propensity to do one of two things when confronted with a need to respond to the terms liberal, con-servative, leftist, and rightist: many citizens do not or cannot respond; but, those who do provide a meaning tend to reflect a common aggregate salience for various definitions of the terms.[12] Voters, non-voters, those engaged and disengaged in politics, liberals, conservatives, leftists, and rightists seem to use the same respective frames of reference when they supply meaning to the core terms in political discourse. Also, compared to the findings of earlier studies, the mass public appears to understand the terms much as they have in the past (Fuchs and Klingemann 1989; Knight 1990; Herrera 1996). This stability of understandings suggests that the public's cognizance of the terms is not influenced greatly by short-term forces.

THE VIEWS OF THE POLITICAL ELITE
AND THE MASS PUBLIC

The United States

In turning to mass–elite communication links, it is clear that the most notable differences between elites and the total sample of the mass public in the United States is in the propensity to supply meaning to the core concepts and the elites' overwhelming usage of abstract terms to define liberal and conservative (see Tables 4.7a and 4.8a).[13] While the mass public tends to employ

[11] In both of these comparisons differences between the groups are significant at $p < 0.05$.

[12] See Herrera (1996), especially the appendix, for a discussion and analysis of the patterns of non-response to the items.

[13] Recall that only the first responses to the questions are used in this analysis. In the survey of delegates a maximum of five responses were coded and in the ANES three responses were coded. The patterns in Tables 4.7a and 4.8a would change if three responses for both samples were used for the analysis but the central finding of elites' almost exclus-ive use of abstract terms would be muted only slightly.

TABLE 4.7a. Aggregate salience of meanings of 'liberal', 1992 US elite and mass samples

Category of response	Elite (%)	Mass (%)	Interested voters (%)	Uninterested non-voters (%)
General philosophy	93	62	61	71
Group references	1	5	6	11
Economic policy	2	12	13	9
Domestic policy	3	17	17	3
Foreign policy	—	1	1	—
Cand/party figure	—	3	3	6
Percentage not responding	23	44	29	79
N	2,204	1,385	1,134	35

Note: Entries are the percentage of respondents whose answers fell into that category. Figures are the percentage of only those responding to the items as are the base numbers of cases.

Source: 1992 American National Election Study, 1992 Convention Delegate Study.

TABLE 4.7b. Aggregate salience of meanings of 'liberal', within the general philosophy category 1992 US elite and mass samples

Category of response	Meaning of 'liberal'		
	Elite (%)	Mass (%)	Interested voters (%)
Change/status quo	14	38	36
Social welfare/free enterprise	51	21	23
Compassionate/uncaring	21	9	9
Independent of/dependent on govt	1	11	9
N	2,044	589	689

Source: 1992 American National Election Study, 1992 Convention Delegate Study.

domestic and economic policy associations to define liberal and conservative', the same is not true for elites. Because of this dominant pattern, we turn to a more refined look at the general philosophical category in the American data (see Tables 4.7b and 4.8b).[14]

---

[14] The American political elite are much more able and willing to respond to the items than the least engaged of the masses. But their non-response was quite comparable, although of different origins and with different meaning, from that of voters. Though these differences in propensity to respond in the American case cannot be dismissed from the larger concern with mass–elite communications linkages, the more telling comparisons may be between those elites and masses who offered their sense of one or another meaning attached

TABLE 4.8*a*. Aggregate salience of meanings of 'conservative', 1992 US elite and mass samples

Category of response	Elite (%)	Mass (%)	Interested voters (%)	Uninterested non-voters (%)
General philosophy	94	63	64	58
Group references	2	7	7	8
Economic policy	2	17	16	23
Domestic policy	2	8	8	3
Foreign policy	—	3	2	3
Cand/party figure	—	3	3	3
Percentage not responding	23	42	27	76
N	2,194	1,442	1,156	40

Note: Entries are the percentage of respondents whose answers fell into that category. Figures are the percentage of only those responding to the items as are the base numbers of cases.
Source: 1992 American National Election Study, 1992 Convention Delegate Study.

TABLE 4.8*b*. Aggregate salience of meanings of 'conservative', within the general philosophy category, 1992 US elite and mass samples

Category of response	Elite (%)	Mass (%)	Interested voters (%)
Change/status quo	19	49	46
Social welfare/free enterprise	47	19	22
Compassionate/uncaring	11	6	5
Independent of/dependent on govt	1	10	9
N	2,051	906	732

Source: 1992 American National Election Study, 1992 Convention Delegate Study.

American political elites differ significantly from the mass public when we take a closer look at the general philosophical response category. Specifically, where the elite tend toward social welfare/free enterprise types of responses, the public associates change/maintenance of the status quo with the two labels respectively.[15] Elites also tend to use references to the compassionate nature of those whose views are liberal and attribute lack of concern for others to conservative beliefs. Though the mass public does not display a misunderstanding of the labels vis-à-vis the political elite, they do

to the conceptual abstractions. The appraisal of congruence between elite and mass understandings of political terminology, consequently, uses respondents to the items as the base for comparisons.

[15] The differences are statistically significant at $p < 0.05$.

differ in the emphasis they place on the dimensions of the ideological terminology. By far, however, the most heavily used definitions of liberal and conservative rely on *either* change/status quo or social welfare/free enterprise understandings (over 60 per cent).

In general, there are many differences between the political elites and the various subgroupings of the American mass public once we take a close look at the types of responses within the general philosophy category. Though the overall similarities among the political elite and interested voters within the mass public are quite impressive with both mass and elite tending to utilize responses that fall into the change/status quo or social welfare/free enterprise category, the magnitude of the differences between mass and elite usage of those two types of responses suggest that communication and representation may be difficult. An elite who associates social welfare and free enterprise when using the labels may have difficulty conversing directly with a mass public who 'hears' change and maintenance of the status quo when the terms are applied.

The Netherlands

Turning to the Dutch case yields virtually no difference between MPs and the mass public in the rate of response to the items and a striking similarity in the understandings of the terms leftist and rightist (see Tables 4.9*a* and 4.10*a*). The first inclination of both voters and members of parliament is to use general philosophic themes to define leftist and rightist with half or more of their responses falling into that category. Though elites are slightly more likely to use group references than the mass public, the category represents the second most used type of response to ascribe meaning to the ideological terms for both groups and the difference is trivial.

A more refined view of the meanings associated by mass and elite within the general philosophy category yields insights similar to yet not as impressive as those found in the American analysis (see Tables 4.9*b* and 4.10*b*). When the Dutch elite use general philosophical responses to ascribe meaning to leftist they tend to mean change and maintenance of the status quo (22 per cent), whereas the mass citizenry associate many meanings to the terms. As expected, those most interested in politics are most similar to the elite, yet even they make more frequent use of social welfare and compassion references than do their representatives.

The understanding of rightist presents more discontinuity between mass and elite. The Dutch electorate, as they did when defining leftist, associates the term with more of the categories listed than do the elites. The Dutch

TABLE 4.9*a*. Aggregate salience of meanings of 'leftist', 1990 Dutch elite and 1994 mass samples

Category of response	Elite (%)	Mass (%)	Very interested (%)	Not very interested (%)
General philosophy	61	79	82	51
Group references	13	13	13	11
Economic policy	1	3	2	1
Domestic policy	2	2	1	2
Foreign policy	1	—	—	—
Cand/party figure	3	3	1	3
Percentage not responding	35	41	15	53
N	137	1,063	208	262

Note: Entries are the percentage of respondents whose answers fell into that category. Figures are the percentage of only those responding to the items as are the base numbers of cases.

Source: 1994 Dutch National Election Study, 1990 Dutch Parliament Study.

TABLE 4.9*b*. Aggregate salience of meanings of 'leftist', within the general philosophy category, 1990 Dutch elite and 1994 mass samples

Category of response	Meaning of 'leftist'		
	Elite (%)	Mass (%)	Interested in politics (%)
Change/status quo	22	15	25
Social welfare/free enterprise	10	20	24
Compassionate/uncaring	5	15	18
Independent of/dependent on govt	2	—	—
N	84	840	171

Source: 1994 Dutch National Election Study, 1990 Dutch Parliament Study.

members of parliament rely heavily on references to independence from government (50 per cent) while the citizenry is more likely to emphasize maintenance of the status quo (18 per cent, 29 per cent) when describing rightist.

Elites and citizens in the United States and the Netherlands share common patterns of discontinuity in the meanings they attach to political terminology. While broad categories of responses indicate great similarity, a more discriminating analysis suggests caution in concluding hastily that elite–mass communication is free from impediments.

TABLE 4.10*a*. Aggregate salience of meanings of 'rightist', 1990 Dutch elite and 1994 mass samples

Category of response	Elite (%)	Mass (%)	Very interested (%)	Not very interested (%)
General philosophy	65	77	75	60
Group references	10	14	13	8
Economic policy	2	4	4	1
Domestic policy	2	1	1	1
Foreign policy	—	—	—	—
Cand/party figure	4	4	5	5
Percentage not responding	36	50	26	56
N	137	1,812	204	265

Note: Entries are the percentage of respondents whose answers fell into that category. Figures are the percentage of only those responding to the items as are the base numbers of cases.

Source: 1994 Dutch National Election Study, 1990 Dutch Parliament Study.

TABLE 4.10*b*. Aggregate salience of meanings of 'rightist', within the general philosophy category, 1990 Dutch elite and 1994 mass samples

Category of response	Elite (%)	Mass (%)	Interested in politics (%)
Change/status quo	22	18	29
Social welfare/free enterprise	6	12	17
Compassionate/uncaring	3	11	15
Independent of/dependent on govt	50	7	11
N	89	1,395	153

Source: 1994 Dutch National Election Study, 1990 Dutch Parliament Study.

Ideologues

Our final comparisons are of the response patterns of self-placed liberals, conservatives, leftists, and rightists among the elite and the mass public (see Tables 4.11*a*, 4.11*b*, 4.12*a*, and 4.12*b*).[16] It is again useful to turn to the more refined categories (see Tables 4.11*b* and 4.12*b*) as the propensity of elites to use general philosophic responses masks important comparisons. One of the more striking patterns is elite conservatives' lack of change/status quo

[16] For the American mass sample, the figures are for interested voters who are self-identified liberals or conservatives.

TABLE 4.11a. Aggregate salience of meanings of ideological counterparts, 1992 US elite and mass samples

Category of response	Meaning of 'liberal'				Meaning of 'conservative'			
	Liberals (%)		Conservatives (%)		Liberals (%)		Conservatives (%)	
	Elite	Mass	Elite	Mass	Elites	Mass	Elites	Mass
General philosophy	94	64	94	56	92	67	96	63
Group references	1	9	1	4	2	11	—	4
Economic policy	1	7	3	15	1	8	3	17
Domestic policy	3	16	2	20	3	8	1	9
Foreign policy	—	—	—	1	1	2	—	2
Cand/party figure	1	—	—	4	—	3	—	4
N	986	297	754	434	982	298	755	434

Note: Entries are the percentage of respondents whose answers fell into that category. The figures for the mass are interested voters who identified as liberal or conservative.

Source: 1992 American National Election Study, 1992 Convention Delegate Study.

TABLE 4.11b. Aggregate salience of meanings of ideological counterparts, within the general philosophy category, 1992 US mass sample

Category of response	Meaning of 'liberal'				Meaning of 'conservative'			
	Liberals (%)		Conservatives (%)		Liberals (%)		Conservatives (%)	
	Elite	Mass	Elite	Mass	Elite	Mass	Elite	Mass
Change/status quo	18	46	6	26	27	56	6	36
Social welfare/free enterprise	32	13	77	32	31	14	74	32
Compassionate/uncaring	31	10	7	8	18	5	2	5
Independence/depend on govt	2	11	1	9	1	10	1	7
N	927	190	709	243	907	200	721	273

Note: Entries are the percentage of respondents whose answers fell into the general philosophy category. The figures for the mass are interested voters who identified as liberal or conservative.

Source: 1992 American National Election Study, 1992 Convention Delegate Study.

Richard Herrera

TABLE 4.12a. Aggregate salience of meanings of ideological counterparts, 1990 Dutch elite and 1994 mass samples

Category of response	Meaning of 'leftist'				Meaning of 'rightist'			
	Leftists (%)		Rightists (%)		Leftists (%)		Rightists (%)	
	Elite	Mass	Elite	Mass	Elite	Mass	Elite	Mass
General philosophy	69	67	43	54	65	50	64	52
Group references	14	12	21	8	14	10	—	9
Economic policy	1	2	—	2	3	3	—	3
Domestic policy	—	1	—	2	—	1	—	1
Foreign policy	—	—	—	—	—	—	—	—
Cand/party figure	1	2	—	4	4	3	—	2
N	71	692	14	683	71	692	14	669

Note: Entries are the percentage of respondents whose answers fell into that category.

Source: 1994 Dutch National Election Study, 1990 Dutch Parliament Study.

The Language of Politics

TABLE 4.12b. Aggregate salience of meanings of ideological counterparts, within the general philosophy category, 1990 Dutch elite and 1994 mass samples

Category of response	Meaning of 'Leftist'				Meaning of 'rightist'			
	Leftists (%)		Rightists (%)		Leftists (%)		Rightists (%)	
	Elite	Mass	Elite	Mass	Elite	Mass	Elite	Mass
Change/status quo	31	20	9	14	24	22	13	16
Social welfare/free enterprise	13	19	4	21	15	19	8	10
Compassionate/uncaring	5	19	4	14	4	16	3	9
Independence/depend on govt	2	—	4	—	57	6	48	6
N	49	464	6	369	46	346	9	348

Note: Entries are the percentage of respondents whose answers fell into the general philosophy category. The figures for the mass are interested voters who identified as liberal or conservative.

Source: 1994 Dutch National Election Study, 1990 Dutch Parliament Study.

references for either liberal or conservative while conservatives at the mass level make frequent use of those references.[17] In addition, conservative elites tend to rely heavily on social welfare-type responses to define liberal (77 per cent) and free enterprise descriptions of conservative (74 per cent) much more than their counterparts in the mass public. Self-described liberals at the elite and mass strata, while using more similar response patterns than conservatives, differ from each other in the former's lack of status quo references to conservative and associations of change with liberal. Curiously, liberal elites' response patterns resemble more closely those of conservatives at the mass level than do the responses of conservative elites. Overall, these discontinuities between self-described ideologues suggest the likelihood of miscommunication between strata of activists. The conclusion that ideologues talk past each other is not quite right since it seems likely that liberal elites may be able to communicate with conservative citizens whereas the reverse is not as likely. It also appears that conservative elites are likely to have difficulty communicating effectively with either liberal or conservatives at the mass level as measured here. In the worst of cases, when they describe a political issue or candidate as liberal or conservative, they apparently mean something vastly different from what the mass public understands by the terms.

The comparison of leftists and rightists in the Dutch case yields more interesting patterns than those found in the previous analysis (see Table 4.12*a*). There is great similarity in the usage of abstract responses to the questions but there are significant differences in the use of other types of responses. Self-described leftists at both levels are most alike with references to groups being a frequently used association for the ideological terms. Elite rightists however, tend to use references to groups much more often (21 per cent) to describe leftists than do voters who describe themselves as rightists (8 per cent). On the other hand, while elite rightists rarely use group references to define rightist, those at the mass level do make use of those associations (9 per cent).[18] The strong overall conclusion from these data are that self-described Dutch leftists and rightists think quite alike when it comes to the terms of ideology and political discourse.

When the general philosophy category is deconstructed (see Table 4.12*b*), dissimilarity is the rule as we compare the responses. The greatest similarity is between self-described leftists who tend to use change/status quo and social welfare/free enterprise when defining both leftist and rightist. For the term rightist, however, there is heavy use of independence from government,

---

[17] The differences are significant at $p < 0.05$.
[18] One should, of course, bear in mind the small numbers of members of parliament who describe themselves as rightists.

(57 per cent) while very few in the mass sample made use of those references (6 per cent).

At a broad level, the parallel images produced by placing the patterns for mass and elite ideologues side by side provide strong evidence that the linkage between the mass public and the political elite, with regard to political terminology, is quite remarkable. Not only do the mass and elite, generally, think about ideological labels in similar ways, important distinctions between self-placed liberals and conservatives remain intact at both levels. The levels of shared understandings of political labels among liberals, conservatives, leftists, and rightists appears to break down when a more intricate inspection of the general philosophy category is made.

CONCLUSION

This study has show that there is considerable agreement between elites and masses (and subgroups among masses) in what I have called the language of politics when broad categories are used to summarize the responses of elite and mass when confronted with political terminology. When we group responses into 'general philosophy' and other types of references, homogeneity of thought is the dominant pattern in both the American and the Dutch data. It is only at this level of categorization, however, that a shared understanding of political language is attained. There is a high degree of slippage among citizens in meanings associated with ideological terms when we move beyond first glances.

While the most problematic of the strata among ordinary citizens are the least engaged politically, even among those engaged in politics, there is a significant minority who do not respond to the abstract terms and who, therefore, may miss elements in elite discussions, debates, and attempts at political leadership. Thus, there is some potential for confusion and misunderstanding, which is particularly troublesome among the inattentive. Given these conditions, it seems likely that elites might 'talk past' some portion of the masses. And, the significant minority of people for whom the terms are irrelevant should not be understated.

While most citizens can understand these terms, how subsets among the masses think about them differ in important ways. Liberals and conservatives in the United States, for instance, differ in the emphasis on the group bases of politics and in the stress placed upon economic policy suggesting that, to some degree, these two groups speak a different political language. In addition, though there is agreement at a broad level, a closer look at those using philosophical responses reveals significant discontinuity among conservatives at the mass and elite levels.

There are no doubt loose couplings in the understanding of the core terms of political debate. Together with the inability of portions of the electorate to comprehend the terminology, the prognosis for good representation in the more detailed and demanding areas of public policy is not bright. Political communication is not simple nor easy, and there is impressive evidence that in addition to the inattentiveness of some of the mass public, misunderstandings between mass and elite are likely to hinder political representation and leadership.

APPENDIX

TABLE 4.A. Aggregate salience of meanings of ideological labels within the general philosophy category, 1992 US mass sample

Category of response	Meaning of 'liberal', mass responding (%)	Meaning of 'conservative', mass responding (%)
Change/status quo	38	49
Social welfare/free enterprise	21	20
Compassionate/uncaring	9	6
Independent of/dependent on govt	11	10
N	859	906

TABLE 4.B. Aggregate salience of meanings of ideological counterparts within the general philosophy category, 1992 US mass sample

Category of response	Meaning of 'liberal'		Meaning of 'conservative'	
	Liberals (%)	Conservatives (%)	Liberals (%)	Conservatives (%)
Change/status quo	46	26	56	36
Social welfare/free enterprise	14	32	14	32
Compassionate/uncaring	10	8	5	5
Independent of/dependent on govt	11	9	10	7
Percentage not responding	54	61	52	56
N	230	289	241	324

Note: Entries are the percentage of respondents whose answers fell into the general philosophy category.

Source: 1992 American National Election Study.

REFERENCES

Conover, Pamela Johnston, and Feldman, Stanley (1981), 'The Origins and Meaning of Liberal/Conservative Self Identification', *American Journal of Political Science*, 25: 617–45.

Converse, Philip E. (1964), 'The Nature of Belief Systems in Mass Publics', in David E. Apter (ed.), *Ideology and Discontent* (New York: Free Press).

Fuchs, Dieter, and Klingemann, Hans-Dieter (1989), 'The Left–Right Schema', in Jennings and van Deth (1989).

Herrera, Cheryl L., Herrera, Richard and Smith, Eric R. A. N. (1992), 'Public Opinion and Congressional Representation', *Public Opinion Quarterly*, 56: 185–205.

Herrera, Richard (1992), 'The Understanding of Ideological Labels by Political Elites: A Research Note', *Western Political Quarterly*, 45: 1021–35.

—— (1996), 'Understanding the Language of Politics: A Study of Elites and Masses', *Political Science Quarterly*, 111 (Winter), 619–37.

—— Epperlein, Thomas, and Smith, Eric R. A. N. (1995), 'The Stability of Congressional Roll-Call Indexes', *Political Research Quarterly*, 48: 403–16.

Inglehart, Ronald (1989), 'Political Value Orientations', in Jennings and van Deth (1989).

Jennings, M. Kent (1993), 'Ideology among Mass Publics and Political Elites', *Public Opinion Quarterly*, 56: 419–41.

—— and van Deth, Jan W. et al. (eds.) (1989), *Continuities in Political Action* (Berlin: Walter de Gruyter).

Kelley, Stanley Jr. (1983), *Interpreting Elections* (Princeton: Princeton University Press).

Kerlinger, Fred N. (1984), *Liberalism and Conservatism: The Nature and Structure of Social Attitudes* (Hillsdale, NJ: Lawrence Erlbaum Associates).

Klingemann, Hans D. (1979a), 'Measuring Ideological Conceptualizations', in Samuel H. Barnes et al., *Political Action* (London: Sage Publications).

—— (1979b), 'The Background of Ideological Conceptualization', in Samuel H. Barnes et al., *Political Action* (London: Sage Publications).

—— (1979c), 'Ideological Conceptualization and Political Action', in Samuel H. Barnes et al., *Political Action* (London: Sage Publications).

Key, V. O. (1961), *Public Opinion and American Democracy* (New York: Alfred A. Knopf).

Knight, Kathleen (1990), 'Ideology and Public Opinion', *Research in Micropolitics*, 3: 59–82.

Levitin, Teresa E., and Miller, Warren E. (1979), 'Ideological Interpretations of Presidential Elections', *American Political Science Review*, 73: 751–71.

McClosky, Herbert (1964), 'Consensus and Ideology in American Politics', *American Political Science Review*, 58: 361–82.

—— and Zaller, John (1984), *The American Ethos* (Cambridge, Mass: Harvard University Press).

—— Hoffmann, Paul J., and O'Hara, Rosemary (1960), 'Issue Conflict and Consensus among Party Leaders and Followers', *American Political Science Review*, 54: 406–27.

Miller, Warren E. (1988), *Without Consent* (Lexington: University of Kentucky Press).

—— and Jennings, M. Kent (1986), *Parties in Transition: A Longitudinal Study of Party Elites and Party Supporters* (New York: Russell Sage Foundation).

—— and Levitin, Teresa E. (1976), *Leadership and Change, Presidential Elections from 1952 to 1976* (Cambridge, Mass.: Winthrop Publishers, Inc.).

Page, Benjamin I., and Shapiro, Robert Y. (1992), *The Rational Public: Fifty Years of Trends in Americans' Policy Preferences* (Chicago: University of Chicago Press).

Prothro, James W., and Grigg, C. W. (1960), 'Fundamental Principles of Democracy: Bases of Agreement and Disagreement', *Journal of Politics*, 22: 276–94.

Smith, Eric R. A. N., Herrera, Richard, and Herrera, Cheryl L. (1990), 'The Measurement Characteristics of Congressional Roll-Call Indexes', *Legislative Studies Quarterly*, 15: 283–95.

van Deth, Jan W. (1983), 'The Persistence of Materialist and Post-Materialist Value Orientations', *European Journal of Political Research*, 11: 63–79.

Zaller, John R. (1992), *The Nature and Origins of Mass Opinion* (Cambridge: Cambridge University Press).

5

Collective Policy Congruence Compared

Sören Holmberg

Parties, not individual parliamentary members or voters, will constitute the principle actors in our analysis. Consequently, we will apply a collectivist model of representation when measuring policy congruence, which means we will study the degree of issue agreement between party voters and party representatives and between all eligible voters and all parliamentary members taken as wholes.

Dyadic representation, focusing on the degree of issue agreement between individual representatives and their constituents, is an alternative approach that perhaps is better suited to the American case, but it will not be pursued in this context since our purpose is to test different party-centred collectivist representation models (Miller and Stokes 1963, Miller 1964, Weissberg 1978, Herrera et al. 1992). Thus, the candidate-centred US system will not be compared to the European systems on its on home turf. The party-centred European systems will have the home advantage; the US system will play the role of the guest team. Consequently, the odds are in favour of the European systems.

Two kinds of analyses of collective policy congruence will be performed. The first is what could be called the conventional method of studying policy congruence, meaning comparisons of attitude means, attitude medians, percentage distributions, or majority positions between elite and mass (McClosky et al. 1960, Eldersveld 1964, Holmberg 1974, Thomassen 1976, Barnes 1977, Huber and Powell 1994, Wessels 1993). The second kind of analysis concentrates on a special aspect of issue agreement between MPs and voters—the extent to which the shape and form of voters' opinion distributions are mirrored by the comparative opinion distributions among members of parliament.

Among statistical buffs, it is a well-known fact that a distribution can not be satisfactory depicted by any single parameter. All the most popular parameters—means, medians, dispersions, skewness, kurtosis—only tell a limited aspect of the total story. By themselves, each can give a very distorted picture of the degree of agreement between two distributions. For example, a bimodal U-shaped distribution can have the same mean as an unimodal A-shaped distribution.

An admittedly crude, but very useful and simple system to classify opinion distributions was designed by Johan Galtung (1969: 234–6). He distinguished between four different shapes that can characterize a distribution: A-curves and J-curves are unimodal with the peak at either end of the scale (J) or toward the middle (A). U-curves are bimodal with the peaks at the ends of the scale while S-curves are multimodal. If the curves are symmetric (or nearly so), Galtung uses a footscript zero, otherwise a + or a − will indicate whether the distribution is skewed to the left or to the right. Accordingly, Galtung's AJUS system permits us to classify distributions in twelve different ways.

An intriguing idea of using the Galtung system, put forward by Warren Miller, would be to see the four different curves as stages in the evolution, if not the maturation, of political issues. J-curves and A-curves represent consensus distributions, while S-curves and especially U-curves, represent polarized opinion curves. By combining the four curves in different sequences opinion formation processes could be modelled. For example, the sequence ASUJ depicts an opinion formation process in which a middle-ground consensus opinion (A) is first polarized (first into an S-curve, then into a U-curve) and then settles down as a new consensus opinion on either extreme (J). The reverse sequence, JUSA, would perhaps be more commonplace in real life; extreme consensus opinions (J-curves) change through public debate and politicization (S- and U-curves) into new compromise opinions toward the middle (A-curves). We will not do much with these ideas in this context since we are focusing on comparative representation, not dynamic representation.

HYPOTHESES

To the extent that system characteristics have an impact on the degree of policy congruence between voters and elected representatives, we would expect political systems with stable and ideological parties, and elections held according to some kind of PR system, to exhibit a closer fit between mass and elite opinions than systems with more catch-all parties and a more individualistic election system. Formulated differently, we expect systems where the responsible party model is the dominant form of governance to show higher degrees of policy congruence between elite and mass than in systems where reponsible parties are not the cornerstones of government (Sartori 1976, Lijpart 1984 and 1994, Shugart and Carey 1992, Daalder and Mair 1983).

Admittedly, responsiveness to voters and issue agreement between voters and leaders are not the defining characteristics of the responsible party model. Accountability to citizens, not responsiveness, is the distinguishing characteristic of the responsible party model (APSA 1950, Wilson 1994, Esaiasson and Holmberg 1996). When despite this we expect a positive relationship between responsible parties and high degrees of policy congruence it is because we expect issue agreement between elite and mass to develop as a side-effect when parties present distinct programmes and make themselves accountable to voters (Klingemann et al. 1994). Issue voting on the part of voters and adherence to programmes on the part of elected representatives should produce policy congruence.

The hypothesis derived from the responsible party model means that we expect that the results on policy congruence between voters and leaders should show highest figures for the European countries, especially for Sweden, with its extreme PR system, strong parties, and egalitarian culture, and maybe excluding France because of its unstable parties and its individualistic election system. For the American case, with its weaker parties, candidate-centred politics, and its plurality voting system, we expect lower degrees of collective policy congruence between voters and elected leaders. The hypothesis pertains to conventional analyses of policy congruence as well as to curve shape analysis.

The shape of opinion distributions is of special interest in party-centred representative systems, since our theoretical notions of parties tell us that in the ideal case within-party opinion profiles on politicized issues should be unimodal; bimodal or multimodal distributions threaten party unity and indicate unsuccessful (or ongoing) opinion forming processes within parties (Sjöblom 1968, Panebianco 1988, Katz and Mair 1995). For extremist parties (on different policy dimensions), we expect J-shaped opinion distributions with peaks at either extreme position, while parties toward the middle on different dimensions are expected to exhibit unimodal opinion curves, albeit with different skewness.

Furthermore, in representative systems where top-down opinion formation is the dominant process on many if not most issues, we should expect party elites (MPs) to reveal more opinion curves of the hypothesized kind, i.e. unimodal J-curves or A-curves, compared to party voters, where we expected to see more erratic multimodal opinion distributions. It takes time, and sometimes it is not possible, for party elites to mould mass opinions; thus voter opinion will not always look the way party elites would like it to. Hence, we should expect to find more multimodal U-shaped or S-shaped opinion profiles among party voters than among party elites.[1]

In the US case, with weaker parties, less issue voting among voters, and an electoral system centred on individual candidates, the expectation should be to find, compared to the European cases, more multimodal opinion distributions among party voters as well as among party elites (Niemi and Westholm 1984, Granberg and Holmberg 1988). The French case, with a more individualistic electoral system and with less stable and cohesive parties than in the other European countries, would be expected to show results somewhere in between the results for the USA and the other three European countries (Converse and Pierce 1986, Pierce 1995a).

If we leave the party level and instead look at the representative system as a whole and compare opinion distributions of all MPs and the entire electorate, our theoretical expectations become less evident. The shape and form of the party system become an important intervening variable. For example, in two-party systems and in multi-party systems with large parties located on the extremes of the dominant dimension, we would expect more U-shaped opinion curves than in one-party dominated systems or in multi-party systems where the large parties are located toward the middle on the most relevant policy dimension. In systems of the latter kind we should expect to find more unimodal opinion distributions. However, seen more broadly and disregarding all nuances, we expect opinion distributions that encompass all MPs or entire electorates to exhibit more multimodal shapes than comparable within-party distributions.

COLLECTIVE POLICY CONGRUENCE

Before we address the more complex analysis of curve shapes and opinion distributions, it is useful to have the outcome of a conventional analysis of policy congruence as a backdrop. Consequently, we start the data presentations by looking at the results of a comparative analysis of collective policy congruence in our five polities. In Tables 5.1 and 5.2, policy congruence between MPs and voters in the Netherlands, United States, West Germany, France, and Sweden have been measured in two different ways; with the help of

---

[1] Dynamic representation, i.e. the interplay over time of opinion formation and decision-making between leaders and voters in a representative democracy, is an emerging new field of research, see Brooks 1990, Page and Shapiro 1992, Stimson et al. 1995, Kuklinski and Segura 1995, Esaiasson and Holmberg 1996, Holmberg 1996, 1997.

the average difference between mean issue positions and with the help of the average summed percentage difference between opinion distributions.[2] Our expectation, derived from the responsible party model, it should be remembered, is that the results should show less policy congruence in the USA than in the European countries.

Contrary to our expectation, however, the results show that the degree of policy congruence does not differ very much between the different political

TABLE 5.1. Issue congruence between MPs and voters in the Netherlands, France, West Germany, the USA, and Sweden

(a)

The Netherlands	Average difference between mean issue positions			Average summed % differences		
	1971/2	1977/9	1989/90	1971/2	1977/9	1989/90
PvdA	1.5	1.1	0.6	46	44	24
D66	1.0	0.9	0.5	48	49	38
CDA	0.9	1.3	1.1	42	42	37
VVD	0.6	1.3	0.6	25	42	27
All	0.8	0.9	0.4	34	35	17
Number of issues	7	5	4	7	5	4

(b)

West Germany	Average difference between mean issue positions 1988/89	Average summed % differences 1988/89
Grüne	0.7	35
SPD	0.6	36
FDP	0.8	29
CDU/CSU	0.8	33
All	0.5	24
Number of issues	12	12

[2] The French data from Converse and Pierce's study from 1967 comprise too few MPs (67) to sustain a reliable analysis of collective policy congruence, especially when the results are broken down by party. In order to strengthen the reliability of the French results on the elite level, I have included all candidates surveyed by Converse and Pierce in the analysis. The total number of interviewed candidates, including 67 elected Deputies, is 232.

(*c*)

USA	Average difference between mean issue positions 1986/7	Average summed % differences 1986/7
Republicans	0.6	30
Democrats	0.7	33
All	0.4	25
Number of issues	8	8

(*d*)

France	Average difference between mean issue positions 1967	Average summed % differences 1967
PCF	1.3	45
Socialists	0.9	33
Centre	1.1	42
Conservatives	0.5	22
Gaullists	0.5	22
All	0.3	20
Number of issues	5	5

Note: The French elite sample is a sample of candidates, not just a sample of elected MPs.

(*e*)

Sweden	Average differences between mean issue positions				Average summed % differences			
	1968/69	1985	1988	1994	1968/69	1985	1988	1994
v	0.9	0.8	0.7	0.7	—	42	39	33
s	0.9	0.8	0.7	0.5	—	33	30	22
c	0.7	0.3	0.4	0.4	—	25	29	27
fp	0.7	0.5	0.6	0.6	—	25	25	28
m	0.6	0.8	0.7	0.9	—	37	32	38
mp	—	—	0.7	0.6	—	—	36	34
kds	—	—	—	0.6	—	—	—	30
All	0.7	0.4	0.3	0.3	—	23	18	16
Number of issues	20	9	12	12	20	9	12	12

Note: The measures of issue congruence are constructed as follows: the means difference measure shows the divergence between members' and voters' opinions when all issue items have been scaled between 1 and 7 (the Netherlands and the USA) or 1 and 5 (West Germany, France, and Sweden), excluding don't knows. The measure can vary between 0.0 (perfect congruence) and 4.0/6.0 (maximum difference). The per cent difference measure is calculated as half the summed difference between members' and voters' percentage distributions, again excluding don't knows. Zero (0) stands for perfect congruence and 100 for maximum policy difference.

TABLE 5.2. Average issue congruence between MPs and voters across major parties in the Netherlands, West Germany, the USA, France, and Sweden as measured by differences of means

| | Number of parties | Averages across parties | |
		Difference between mean issue positions	Summed % differences
The Netherlands			
1971/2	4	1.0	43
1977/9	4	1.2	44
1989/90	4	0.7	32
West Germany			
1988/9	4	0.7	32
USA			
1986/7	2	0.7	32
France			
1967	5	0.9	33
Sweden			
1968/9	5	0.8	—
1985	5	0.6	32
1988	6	0.6	32
1994	7	0.6	30

Note: The party results in Table 5.2 have been summed and averaged across 4 parties in the Netherlands and West Germany, across 2 parties in the USA, across 5 parties in France, and across 5/6/7 parties in Sweden.

parties or between the five nations. The extent of issue agreement between MPs and voters is about the same in the Netherlands, the USA, Germany, France, and Sweden. The fact that the results for some of the Dutch studies reveal somewhat lower levels of policy congruence could have a methodological explanation. The Dutch (and American) studies used 7-point scales when they measured issue positions while the German and Swedish studies used 5-point scales and the French study applied a 4-point scale. This means that, for example, the measure for the difference between means can vary between 0 and 4 in Sweden and Germany, but between 0 and 6 in the Netherlands and in the USA. Given this disparity between measurement scales and the limited number of issues involved, the safest conclusion is that the (early) Dutch results probably do not indicate lower levels of policy congruence than in the other countries.

This conclusion is underscored by the fact that the USA results (based on 7-point scales) and the results for the latest Dutch Study (in 1989/90) indicate about the same level of average issue agreement as in Sweden, France, and Germany.[3] As a matter of fact, if we standardize our measures, taking into account the differences in the scales used, the level of policy congruence turns out to be slightly higher in the US and the (latest) Dutch studies than in the German, the French, and the Swedish studies. Transformed to a scale running from 0 (high congruence) to 1 (low congruence), the policy congruence between all members and the entire electorate would be 0.066 for the Netherlands and the USA, 0.075 for Sweden and France, and 0.125 for Germany.[4]

However, as was stated before, the differences between the country results on this standardized scale should not be played up. Given the differences in measurement techniques and measurement scales and the very limited number of issues included in some studies, the conservative conclusion is that the degree of collective policy congruence between elected leaders and voters did not differ in any substantial way between the five political systems. Hence, our hypothesis derived from the responsible party model has been disproved. Collective policy congruence between politicians and voters is not higher in party-dominated European political systems than in the candidated-centred and more individualistic American system. And within Europe, issue agreement did not prove to be lower in France with its unstable party system and plurality voting system than in the more stable and PR-oriented systems of the Netherlands, Sweden, and Germany. Thus, our conventional analysis of policy congruence between elite and mass could not prove that the political system matters. On the contrary, it indicated that the political system does not matter when it comes to degrees of policy congruence between leaders and voters in Western democracies.

[3] In the early 1970s, Charles Backstrom studied collective policy congruence in the USA, using six different issue questions. He found higher degrees of congruence between House members and the public than between Senators and the public, but overall the level of policy congruence was about the same as in Sweden; see Backstrom 1977: 411–35 and Holmberg 1989: 1–36.

[4] Standardizing is always a tricky business, and eminently so in this case. The question is if it is at all possible through standardization to neutralize the fact that voters and members of parliaments in the five studied countries were presented with different-numbered issue scales (4-point, 5-point, and 7-point scales). In doing the standardization, the French 4-point scale was first transformed to a 1–5 scale (coded 1, 2, 4, 5), excluding the don't knows. Bernhard Wessels uses a slightly different standardized measure of collective policy congruence in his chapter. According to Wessels measure the countries could be rank ordered in the following manner from high to low degrees of policy congruence: the Netherlands 6.9, the USA 8.4, Sweden 9.6, France 11.1, and Germany 13.7. As can be readily seen Wessels' rank ordering is in concurrence with mine.

CURVE SHAPE ANALYSIS

The similarities between the results of a conventional congruence analysis for our five political systems make the curve shape investigation the more interesting. Maybe studying opinion distributions will reveal more differences between parties and political systems.

The curves in figures 5.1 and 5.2 serve an illustrative purpose. They give a feel for how much more rewarding and revealing looking at opinion profiles can be, compared to inspecting means or dispersion measures, and how useful, albeit crude, the AJUS system is.

The left–right curves in figure 5.1 are based on self-placements made by Social Democratic MPs and voters in the European countries and by Democratic congressmen and voters in the USA, and demonstrate once more the old finding that leftist/liberal elite groups tend to locate themselves further to the left than leftist/liberal voters. All curves are A-shaped—with the exception of the French S-shaped curve among voters—and skewed to the left. It is worth noting, however, that the Dutch voter distribution is rather close to a left-leaning J-curve. Among Dutch PvdA voters, 18 per cent locate themselves to the far left (1 on the scale), compared to 0 per cent among socialist MPs. The majority of Dutch PvdA members tend to locate themselves a little more toward the middle, at scale point 2 (53 per cent).

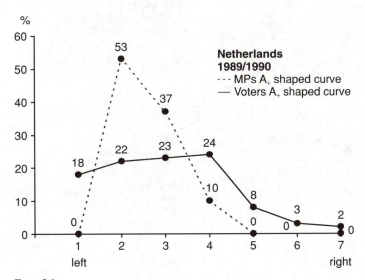

FIG. 5.1.

Sören Holmberg

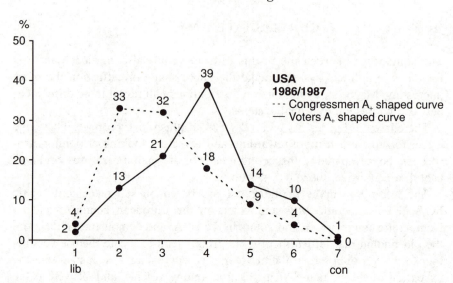

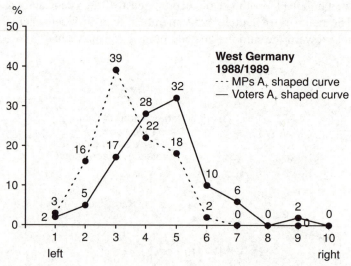

FIG. 5.1.

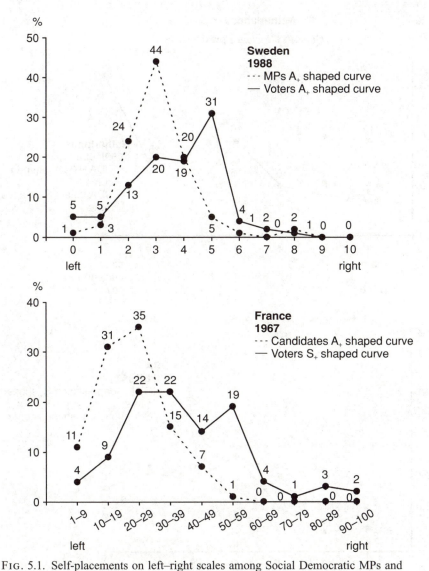

FIG. 5.1. Self-placements on left–right scales among Social Democratic MPs and voters in France, the Netherlands, West Germany, and Sweden: self-placement on a liberal-conservative scale among Democratic congressmen and voters in the USA

Note: The US result is based on data from the American National Election Study of 1986 and a Congressional Study (House of Representatives) performed by Rick Herrera in 1987. The German data is from the German Representation Study of 1988/9 (Wessels 1994) and the Dutch data from the Dutch Representation Study of 1989/90 (Horstman and Thomassen 1994). The French data comes from Converse and Pierce's Representation Study of 1967. The Swedish Representation Study of 1988 has provided the Swedish data. An A. shaped curve is a unimodal curve titled to the left.

Sören Holmberg

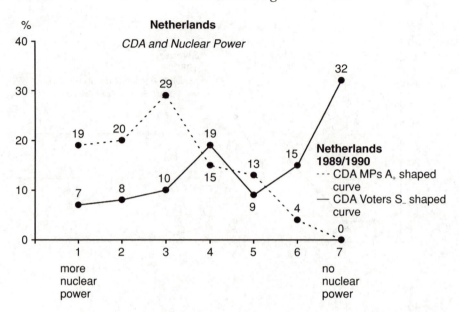

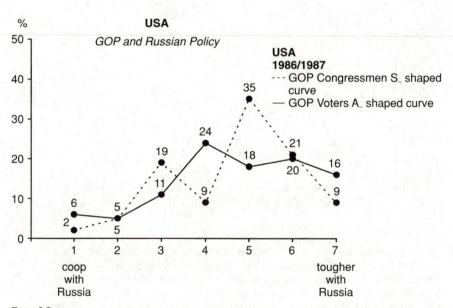

Fig. 5.2.

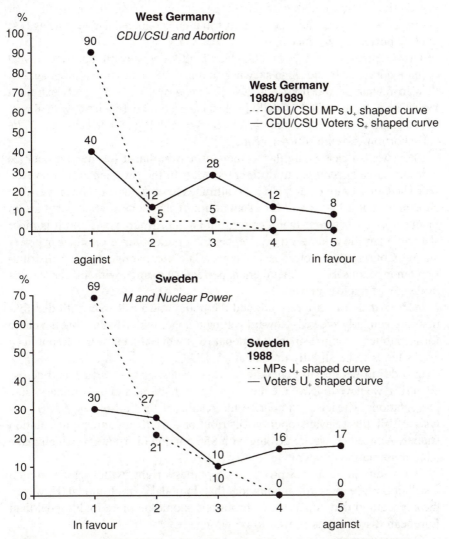

FIG. 5.2. AJUS-analysis of elite and mass opinion curves in the Netherlands, West Germany, the USA, and Sweden

Note: A₊ shaped curves are unimodal and titled to the left. J₊ curves are also unimodal and titled to the left. S curves are multimodal and skewed to the right (S₋), to the left (S₊), or to the middle (S₀). U₊ curves are bimodal and leaning to the left.

The results in figure 5.2 illustrate cases where the shape and skewness of opinion distributions overlap less. In the case of the Dutch CDA party and the opinion on nuclear power, both shape and skewness are different when we compare the within-party opinion profiles of MPs and voters. The member distribution is unimodal with an emphasis on support for more nuclear power (an A_+ curve), while the voter distribution is bimodal and leaning against nuclear power (an S_- curve).

The German case of CDU/CSU and attitudes toward abortion reveal opinion curves with the same skewness among MPs and voters (more against than in favour of abortion) but different shapes; CDU/CSU MPs exhibit a very clear J-curve while CDU/CSU voters have a bimodal S-curve, with almost as many persons locating themselves in the middle (28 per cent) as to the anti-abortion extreme (40 per cent).

The Swedish case is similar to the German in that it too involves curves with the same skewness but different shapes. In the Swedish case, however, with the Conservative party (M) and attitudes toward nuclear power, we have an example of a U-curve. More supporters of the Conservative party are in favour of nuclear power than against, but an anti-group exists and it is more sizeable than the middle group. Hence, the opinion curve on nuclear power among Conservative voters is U-shaped. The comparable opinion distribution among Conservative members is perfectly J-shaped with a clear leaning in favour of nuclear power.

In the American case of GOP and the policy toward Russia both distributions are similarly skewed—toward getting tougher with Russia—but the curve for Republican congressmen is bimodal (S_-) while the curve for Republican voters tends to be slightly unimodal (A_-).[5]

In order to be able to generalize across issues, across parties, and across countries, we have to leave the nice curve presentations and use ordinary table presentations when we summarize the results of the full-blown AJUS analysis of all the relevant opinion distributions from our ten representation studies. Altogether, we are dealing with 856 opinion distributions which make table presentations imperative.

The results in Table 5.3 prove our hypothesis right; within-party opinion distributions are more often unimodal than bimodal or multimodal. However, the expectation that American distributions should be more multimodal than European distributions proved to be wrong.

Among members in all five countries and among voters in Sweden, Germany, and the USA opinion curves were more often unimodal than multimodal. In the Netherlands, opinion profiles among voters tend to be somewhat more multimodal; half of the opinion curves among Dutch voters were multimodel, the other half unimodal. The French result for the voters deviate completely. In France, within-party opinion distributions among voters are most often multimodal.

[5] The American data is from the late 1980s, i.e. Russia stands for the old Soviet Union.

TABLE 5.3. Within-party issue profiles among MPs and voters in the USA, the Netherlands, West Germany, France, and Sweden

Issue profile	Netherlands		West Germany		Sweden		USA		France	
	MPs	Voters	MPs	Voters	MPs	Voters	MPs	Voters	MPs	Voters
A	59	27	31	52	40	43	75	63	12	0
J	19	23	35	27	53	25	0	12	64	28
U	0	5	0	0	1	1	0	0	12	16
S	22	45	34	21	6	31	25	25	12	56
sum percentage	100	100	100	100	100	100	100	100	100	100
number of cases	64	64	48	48	201	201	16	16	25	25
per cent unimodal (A+J)	78	50	66	79	93	68	75	75	76	28
per cent multimodal (U+S)	22	50	34	21	7	32	25	25	24	72

Note: AJUS-analysis is a simplified technique designed to study statistical distributions like MPs' or voters' issue profiles. A and J stand for unimodal distributions with the peak in either end of the scales (J) or toward the middle (A). U-curves are bimodal with the peaks at the end of the scales while S-curves are multimodal. Within-party issue profiles among MPs and voters are the focus of the analysis. The Dutch data are based on the Representation Studies of 1971/2 (4 parties, 7 issues = 28 cases), 1977/9 (4 parties, 5 issues = 20 cases), and 1989/90 (4 parties, 4 issues = 16 cases); in total 64 cases. The West German data draw on the Representation Study 1988/9 (4 parties, 12 issues = 48 cases). The American results come from a Representation Study in 1986/7 (2 parties, 8 issues = 16 cases). The French results are based on Converse and Pierce's Representation Study from 1967 (5 parties, 5 issues = 25 cases). The Swedish results are based on the Representation Studies of 1985 (5 parties, 9 issues = 45 cases), 1988 (6 parties, 12 issues = 72 cases), and 1994 (7 parties, 12 issues = 84 cases); in total 201 cases.

Our expectation that members of parliaments should exhibit more cohesive policy attitudes than voters is clearly upheld in the Netherlands, France, and Sweden. Within parties, MPs exhibit more unimodal opinion distributions than voters. The Swedish case is especially pronounced with 93 per cent of all within-party opinion profiles shaped as unimodal A-curves or J-curves among MPs. The comparable outcome among Swedish voters is 68 per cent. In the German case, results are reversed with voters, contrary to expectations, exhibiting more unimodal opinion distributions then MPs, while in America, congressmen as well as voters showed the same result, 75 per cent unimodal curves vs. 25 per cent multimodal.

One reason for the rather clear outcome in the Swedish case could be the dominance of the left–right dimension in Swedish politics (and consequently also of left–right issues in our questionnaires). For example, among MPs of the Left party, 85 per cent of all opinion distributions were shaped as J-curves leaning to the left. On the other end of the left–right continuum, among Conservative MPs, 73 per cent of all opinion profiles were also J-shaped, although leaning to the right. In the middle, among Liberal MPs, as expected, the opinion distributions were dominated by unimodal A-curves (67 per cent).

The results in Table 5.4, pertaining to parliaments and electorates as wholes, lend support to the hypothesis that within-party opinion distributions tend to be more unimodal than distributions involving all MPs or the entire electorate. As a matter of fact, the hypothesis is strongly supported in our material. In all five countries, and among voters as well as among members, within-party opinion profiles are unimodal to a larger extent than among all MPs or all eligible voters.

The results for the Swedish members are the best case in point. Within-party, 93 per cent of all opinion curves among Swedish MPs were unimodally shaped, while only 7 per cent had a multimodal form. When we study all MPs, the results get reversed with only 48 per cent unimodal curves versus 52 per cent multimodal curves (most often U-curves).

In the Netherlands, studying all MPs, the pattern is the same although the proportion of the more consensual unimodal opinion distributions is higher among Dutch MPs than among Swedish MPs. Among Dutch and American members, we could not find a single U-shaped opinion curve. Among Swedish MPs and French Candidates we found 34 and 60 per cent, respectively (8 per cent among German members).

On the voter level U-shaped distributions were extremely rare, 20 per cent among French voters, 6 per cent among Dutch voters, and 0 per cent among the voters in the other countries. Hence, Swedish and French MPs are the conflictful outliers characterized by a large proportion of U-shaped opinion distributions. American congressmen come close in the sense that a clear

TABLE 5.4. Issue profiles among all MPs and the entire electorate

Issue Profile	Netherlands		Sweden		West Germany		USA		France	
	MPs	Electorate	MPs	Electorate	MPs	Electorate	House	Electorate	Candidates	Electorate
A	37	19	21	43	34	42	37	63	0	0
J	19	25	27	18	8	25	0	0	40	20
U	0	6	34	0	8	0	0	0	60	20
S	44	50	18	39	50	33	63	37	0	60
sum percentage	100	100	100	100	100	100	100	100	100	100
number of cases	16	16	33	33	12	12	8	8	5	5
per cent unimodal (A+J)	56	44	48	61	42	67	37	63	40	20
per cent multimodal (U+S)	44	56	52	39	58	33	63	37	60	80

Note: The France results are based on a sample of voters and candidates, not on MPs and a sample of the entire electorate.

TABLE 5.5. Correspondence of within-party profiles between MPs and voters in the Netherlands, West Germany, France, Sweden, and the USA

	Netherlands	West Germany	Sweden	USA	France
Corresponding issue profiles	26	40	41	50	40
Same form, different skewness	17	8	10	12	0
Same skewness, different form	41	27	36	25	40
Different form and different skewness	16	25	13	13	20
sum percentage	100	100	100	100	100
number of cases	64	48	201	16	25

Note: In AJUS-analysis, the focus or skewness of the distributions is classified as + (leaning toward the left), 0 (focus toward the middle), and – (leaning toward the right). The form of the distributions is designated as either A, J, U or S.

majority of their opinion curves also were bimodal (63 per cent), but of S-shapes rather than U-shapes.

The outcome of a curve shape analysis of within-party policy congruence between MPs and voters is presented in Table 5.5.

The degree of correspondence between members' and voters' opinion distributions is classified in four categories—Corresponding issue profiles (the same shape and skewness), Same shape but different skewness, Same skewness but different shape, and Different shape as well as different skewness. The Swedish, French, and German cases exhibit about the same proportion of completely corresponding within-party opinion distributions between MPs and voters (40 per cent), while the Dutch result reveal a somewhat lower percentage of corresponding distributions (26 per cent). The American result comes out as number one with 50 per cent of all within-party distributions showing a complete correspondence between the opinion profiles of congressmen and the opinion profiles of their parties' supporters.

The German case demonstrates the highest number of totally different within-party opinion distributions between members and voters (25 per cent). The comparable results in Sweden, France, the USA, and the Netherlands are somewhat better—13, 20, 13, and 16 per cent, respectively.

The main conclusion of our curve shape analysis of policy congruence is roughly the same as the one we made earlier based on the conventional study of issue agreement between MPs and voters in the five countries; policy congruence looks about the same in all five systems. Comparing the American and the European results, it is apparent that the American system, different as it is on many counts from the European systems, did not produce dramatically

TABLE 5.6. Correspondence of issue profiles between all MPs and the entire electorates in the Netherlands, the USA, Sweden, France, and West Germany

	Netherlands	West Germany	Sweden	USA	France
Corresponding issue profiles	37	42	27	13	20
Same form, different skewness	6	8	3	37	0
Same skewness, different form	38	17	40	25	60
Different form and different skewness	19	33	30	25	20
sum percentage	100	100	100	100	100
number of cases	16	12	33	8	5

different levels of policy congruence between leaders and voters. There are more similarities than differences, even if the curve shape analysis revealed more differences than the conventional analysis.

The results in Table 5.6, involving a comparison of all MPs with entire electorates, is a good case in point. They highlight what we already saw earlier. The correspondence of issue profiles between MPs and voters does not differ in any drastic way across our five political systems. Although, the proportion of completely corresponding curves between members and voters was somewhat higher in the Netherlands (37 per cent) and in Germany (42 per cent) than in Sweden (27 per cent), in France (20 per cent), or in the USA (13 per cent). The main reason for this difference was revealed earlier by the AJUS analysis. Among American congressmen S-curves, sometimes bordering on U-curves, were relatively frequent. Among Swedish and French leaders, clear bimodal U-shaped opinion distributions were quite common (34 and 60 per cent, respectively). Among members in the other countries and among voters in all countries U-curves were extremely rare. Opinion distributions among all leaders in Sweden, France, and the USA differed more from the opinion distributions among voters than was the case in the Netherlands and Germany.

A possible conclusion is that the Swedish and French representative systems, and perhaps also the American system, are characterized by more polarization and conflict among MPs than among voters, and that the Dutch and German systems are more consensual. Given the fact that we are dealing with a limited number of studies, partly different methodologies, and a small sample of issues in most cases, the conclusion must be highly tentative. Especially, since none of our hypotheses predicted the outcome and it is difficult to see what kind of political or institutional factors would explain the result. Still more representation studies are needed before we can draw any more general conclusions.

Curve shape analysis is more rewarding to perform than ordinary difference of means analysis and it is an absolute must in systems with polarized or erratic opinion distributions. Traditional difference of means studies of policy congruence are permissible in well-behaved systems characterized by a dominance of J- and A-shaped opinion curves. When things get heated up, and S-shaped and U-shaped opinion curves start to appear, we need the assistance of curve shape analysis.

THE RESPONSIBLE PARTY MODEL ASSESSED

Comparing our results between America and Europe, or between the systems with strong parties and parliamentary rule (the Netherlands, Sweden, and Germany) and the systems with weaker parties, a mixture of presidential and parliamentary rule and individualistic election systems (France and the USA), it is evident that the similarities are more apparent than the differences. Granted that we found some differences, for example more polarized attitudes among elites than among voters in Sweden, the USA, and France compared to the Netherlands and Germany, the dominant pattern, especially taking into account the very few issues studied and the limited number of MPs interviewed in some cases, is that policy congruence between voters and leaders does not tend to be higher in systems where the responsible party model is the dominant model of governance (Sweden, Germany, and the Netherlands) than in the USA and France, where more mixed systems of governance are used. This means that our hypothesis has been disproved. We expected the responsible party model to excel and it did not. The individualistic American system produced the same degree of collective issue agreement between elite and mass as the more collectivist and party-dominated European systems.

A speculative reason as to why the responsible party model, in its European version, seems to have failed to deliver higher degrees of policy congruence, is the presence of a strong tendency to political leadership on the part of elites combined with poor showings when it comes to opinion moulding. A critical way of summing up our findings is to acknowledge that the level of issue agreement between voters and leaders is not especially high; on the contrary, it is rather poor. In the Swedish case, a Riksdag chosen by lot in a totally random fashion, without resorting to the costly and time-consuming procedures of candidate nominations, election campaigns, and popular voting, would almost always produce higher degrees of policy congruence than the ones we have found in our empirical studies. The probability of getting the kind of average summed per cent differences between elite and mass opinions, as we found in 1968, 1985, 1988, and 1994, if members were chosen randomly, is very small, less than one in a thousand. Since the congruence results for the Netherlands, France, Germany, and the USA were very similar in degrees to the result for Sweden, it is obvious that lottery procedures would outperform the representative processes in those countries as well.

Consequently, on a normative level, our results are not altogether satisfying. Policy leadership does not only imply being ahead of the voters, it also implies opinion moulding and trying to bring the people along. Low levels of policy congruence and more conflictful elites than voters, in systems with issue voting citizens, not only imply dangers to individual parties and candidates, they also imply dangers for the representative system as a whole. The increased levels of distrust in parties and politicians, the downward trend in turnout, and the decreased levels of party identification in many Western democracies are signs that should be taken seriously.[6]

Representative democracy is a delicate system basically built on trust and a fine-tuned balance between political leadership and responsiveness. Too much leadership leads to elitism, too much responsiveness leads to populism. If anything, the results from our ten representation studies indicate that the scale is somewhat unbalanced in all countries represented in our study. Political leadership and representation run from above carries more weight than responsiveness and representation run from below.

REFERENCES

APSA (1950), 'Toward a More Responsible Two-Party System', *American Political Science Review*, 44 (Suppl.), 1–99.

Backstrom, C. H. (1977), 'Congress and the Public: How representative is one of the other?' *American Political Science Quarterly*, 5: 411–35.

Barnes, S. H. (1977), *Representation in Italy: Institutionalized Tradition and Electoral Choice* (Chicago: University of Chicago Press).

---

[6] In Klingemann and Fuchs (1995) useful time series and comparative studies of turnout (Topf), political trust (Listhaug), and party identification (Schmitt and Holmberg) can be found. Most of the analyses deal with European data from the post-war period, especially from the period between the late 1960s and early 1990s. A comparative study of party identification in Europe and America can also be found in Holmberg 1994.

Brooks, J. (1990), 'The Opinion–Policy Nexus in Germany', *Public Opinion Quarterly*, 54: 208–29.

Converse, P., and Pierce, R. (1986), *Political Representation in France* (Cambridge, Mass.: Harvard University Press).

Daalder, H., and Mair, P. (eds.) (1983), *Western European Party Systems: Continuity & Change* (London: Sage).

Eldersveld, S. J. (1964), *Political Parties: A Behavioral Analysis* (Chicago: Rand McNally).

Esaiasson, P., and Holmberg, S. (1996), *Representation from above: Members of Parliament and Representative Democracy in Sweden* (Aldershot: Dartmouth).

Galtung, J. (1969), *Theory and Methods of Social Research* (Oslo: Universitets-forlaget).

Granberg, D., and Holmberg, S. (1988), *The Political System Matters: Social Psychology and Voting Behavior in Sweden and the United States* (Cambridge: Cambridge University Press).

Herrera, C., Herrera, R., and Smith, E. (1992), 'Public Opinion and Congressional Representation', *Public Opinion Quarterly*, 56: 185–205.

Herrera, R. (1994), 'Mass Sample NES 1986/Congress Sample 1987' (Department of Political Science, Arizona State University).

Holmberg, S. (1974), *'Riksdagen representerar svenska folket': Empiriska studier i representativ demokrati* (Lund: Studentlitteratur).

—— (1989), 'Political Representation in Sweden', *Scandinavian Political Studies*, 12: 1–36.

—— (1994), 'Party Identification Compared across the Atlantic', in K. Jennings and T. Mann (eds.), *Elections at Home and Abroad: Essays in Honor of Warren E. Miller* (Ann Arbor: University of Michigan Press).

—— (1996), 'Svensk åsiktsöverensstämmelse', in B. Särlvik and B. Rothstein (eds.), *Vetenskapen om politik: festskrift till professor emiritus Jörgen Westerståhl* (Göteborg: Statsvetenskapliga institutionen).

—— (1997), 'Dynamic Opinion Representation', *Scandinavian Political Studies*, 20: 265–83.

Horstman, R., and Thomassen, J. (1994), 'Distribution of Issue Positions and General Orientations of MPs and Voters: Dutch Representation Study 1972/1979/1990' (Department of Public Administration, Twente University).

Huber, J., and Powell, B. (1994), 'Congruence between Citizens and Policymakers in Two Visions of Liberal Democracy', *World Politics*, 46: 291–326.

Katz, R., and Mair, P. (1995), 'Changing Models of Party Organization and Democracy: The Emergence of the Cartel Party', *Party Politics*, 1: 5–28.

Klingemann, H. D., and Fuchs, D. (eds.) (1995), *Citizens and the State* (Oxford: Oxford University Press).

—— Hofferbert, R., and Budge, I. (1994), *Parties, Policies and Democracy* (Boulder, Colo.: Westview Press).

Kuklinski, J., and Segura, G. (1995), 'Endogeneity, Exogeneity, Time and Space in Political Representation', *Legislative Studies Quarterly*, 20: 3–21.

Lijpart, A. (1984), *Democracies: Patterns of Majoritarian and Consensus Government in Twenty-One Countries* (New Haven: Yale University Press).

—— (1994), *Electroral Systems and Party Systems: A Study of Twenty-Seven Democracies, 1945–1990* (Oxford: Oxford University Press).

McClosky, H., Hoffman, P., and O'Hara, R. (1960), 'Issue Conflict and Consensus among Party Leaders and Followers', *American Political Science Review*, 54: 406–27.

Miller, W. E. (1964), 'Majority Rule and the Representative System of Government', in E. Allardt and Y. Littunen (eds.), *Cleavages, Ideologies and Party Systems: Contributions to Comparative Political Sociology* (Helsinki: Academic Bookstore).

—— and Stokes, D. E. (1963), 'Constituency Influence in Congress', *American Political Science Review*, 57: 45–56.

Niemi, R., and Westholm, A. (1984), 'Issues, Parties and Attitudinal Stability: A Comparative Study of Sweden and the United States', *Electoral Studies*, 3: 65–83.

Page, B., and Shapiro, R. (1992), *The Rational Public: Fifty Years of Trends in Americans' Policy Preferences* (Chicago: University of Chicago Press).

Panebianco, A. (1988), *Political Parties: Organization and Power* (Cambridge: Cambridge University Press).

Pierce, R. (1995*a*), *Choosing the Chief: Presidential Elections in France and the United States* (Ann Arbor: University of Michigan Press).

—— (1995*b*), 'France 1967: Mass and Elite Issue Scale Positions by Five Party Groups' (Institute for Social Research, University of Michigan).

Sartori, G. (1976), *Parties and Party Systems: A Framework for Analysis* (Cambridge: Cambridge University Press).

Shugart, M. and Carey, J. (1992), *Presidents and Assemblies: Constitutional Design and Electoral Dynamics* (Cambridge: Cambridge University Press).

Sjöblom, G. (1968), *Party Strategies in a Multiparty System* (Lund: Student-litteratur).

Stimson, J., MacKuen, M., and Erikson, R. (1995), 'Dynamic Representation', *American Political Science Review*, 89: 543–65.

Thomassen, J. (1976), *Kiezers en gekozenen in een representatieve demokratie* (Alphen aan den Rijn: Samson).

Weissberg, R. F. (1978), 'Collective vs Dyadic Representation in Congress', *American Political Science Review*, 72: 535–47.

Wessels, B. (1993), 'Politische Repräsentation: Kommunikation als Transmissionssiemen alter und never Politik', in D. Herzog, H. Rebenstorf, and B. Wessels (eds.), *Parlament und Gesellschaft: Eine Funktionsanalyse der Repräsentativen Demokratie* (Opladen: Westdeutscher Verlag).

—— (1994), 'Distribution of Issue Positions and General Political Orientations of MPs and Voters: German Representation Study 1988/1989' (Berlin: Wissenschaftszentrum).

Wilson, G. (1994), 'The Westminster Model in Comparative Perspective', in I. Budge and D. McKay (eds.), *Developing Democracy* (London: Sage).

6

Not All Politics is Local
The Geographical Dimension of Policy Representation

Peter Esaiasson

Americans and Europeans tend to think differently about political representation. Traditionally, US political scientists view the process of political representation as individualistic and local. Elected representatives are independent political entrepeneurs who are responsible only to their own particular geographical constituency.[1] In contrast, European political scientists perceive the process of representation as party collectivistic and national. Elected representatives are collective actors who are committed to a national party programme and are responsible to a national constituency.[2] In what follows, these two different views of political representation are referred to as the local approach and the party-collective approach, respectively.[3]

In preparing the data for this analysis I have received a lot of help from fellow participants in this project Roy Pierce (France), Rick Herrerra (the USA), and Bernhard Wessels (West Germany). Thanks also to Jan Flickschu of Wissenschaftszentrum Berlin and Sophie Johansson of Göteborg University. The analysis is influenced by ideas laid out in a working paper by Warren Miller and Bo Särlvik 'National vs Constituency Representation in Sweden' (1975), which they generously shared with me. In addition to comments from participants in the project, I have benefited from suggestions made by John Geer, Mikael Gilljam, Knut Heidar, and Bo Reimer.

[1] Defining studies in the tradition are Miller and Stokes (1963); Mayhew (1974); and Fenno (1978).

[2] Thomassen's (1991) critique of the Miller–Stokes Diamond Model is a case in point.

[3] The terminology of the field is somewhat shifting. What is here called 'the local approach' is often labelled 'the dyadic model' (Weissberg 1978) or 'the delegate model' (Thomassen in this volume). I have chosen 'the local approach' rather than 'dyadic representation' because the latter refers to the US type of linkage between constituents and one specific representative, whereas in this comparative framework 'local linkages' sometimes refers to linkages between constituents and a group of specific representatives. The term 'delegate model' is not appropriate because it implies a bottom-up type of linkage between constituents and representatives. For this particular purpose at least, it is not necessary to make this assumption. As will become clear, a local linkage might just as well be established by representatives who shape local public opinion.

Given the differences that exist in electoral arrangements, it may seem natural that different approaches have developed. Americans and Europeans have simply chosen an approach to representation that is useful in their own political setting. However, to concede easily that one approach is as useful as the other is hardly intellectually satisfying. A more challenging endeavour is to try to assess the validity of the respective approaches in various electoral contexts. The goal of this study is to make such an assessment.

Differences notwithstanding, electoral systems operate similarly enough for proponents of either to have confidence in their own approach. Those who pursue the local approach to political representation can stress that representatives are formally tied to a specific geographical constituency in almost all electoral systems. To further strenghthen their case, the important nomination process tends to be decentralized in most systems; local party organizations and other protagonists watch jealously over their right to decide who their representatives will be (e.g. Gallagher and Marsh 1988). Since most electoral systems share these basic characteristics, it is not surprising that in recent years US political scientists have been looking for linkages between constituents and specific representatives in as varying national set-ups as Costa Rica (Taylor 1992); Denmark (Patterson 1991); France (Converse and Pierce 1986); Israel (Uslaner 1985); the UK (e.g. Cain et al. 1987); and West Germany (Lancaster and Patterson 1990).

Correspondingly, proponents of the party-collectivistic approach to political representation can argue that the process of opinion formation tends to be nationalized in most Western nations. Even in the federal and individualistic American political system, voters are likely to relate to national figureheads who are tied to a particular party rather than to local politicians (e.g. Kuklinski and Segura 1995; cf. Weissberg 1978). To the extent that the conduct of voters and representatives is driven by national forces, the dyadic (local) linkage between constituents and specific representatives is reduced to a formality. Indeed, proponents of the collectivistic approach claim that many US political scientists are moving in their direction. In recent years several studies have looked for linkages between aggregate public opinion and policy enacted rather than for dyadic linkages between local constituents and their specific representative (e.g. Bartels 1991; Page and Shapiro 1992; Stimson et al. 1995; Wlezien 1996).

An assessment of the validity of the two approaches may begin with the generally acknowledged circumstance that political representation is a multifaceted phenomenon. In a well-known typology, Eualu and Karps (1977) suggest that political representation can be thought of in terms of four components of responsiveness: service, allocation, policy, and symbolic responsiveness. *Service* responsiveness refers to the willingness of representatives to do favours for individual constituents (representatives as errand boys). *Allocation* responsiveness involves the willingness of representatives to secure public benefits for a particular geographical constituency. *Policy* responsiveness refers to interactions between representatives and their constituents with respect to the making of public policy. *Symbolic* responsiveness, finally, concerns the sense of trust and support in the relationship between representative and represented. Using the logic of such reasoning, it can be argued that the two approaches emphasize different aspects of political representation. The local approach tends to give high priority to *service* and *allocation* responsiveness, whereas the party-collectivistic approach is mainly concerned with *policy* responsiveness and *symbolism*.[4]

With regards to service and allocation responsiveness, there are indications that by concentrating on parties as collective actors, European political scientists have been overlooking important linkages between citizens and their elected representatives. Available evidence indicates that throughout the Western world MPs are concerned with the promotion of their constituency's interests. For example, the above-mentioned studies by US political scientists have been at least partly successful in their search for electoral connections in non-American settings (Lancaster and Patterson 1990; Patterson 1991; Cain et al. 1987; Uslaner 1985; Taylor 1992). Confirming this conclusion, a systematic study of the Swedish case, where parliamentary parties are as disciplined as anywhere in Europe, found that virtually every elected representative acted as a local promoter during parliamentary sessions and that local initiatives were especially frequent during election years (Esaiasson and Holmberg 1996; Roth 1996). Furthermore, when a group of country specialists were brought together to give their best assessments of MP–constituency linkages, they reported that Western representatives keep in contact with their geographical constituencies in a number of ways (Bogdanor 1984).[5]

---

[4] This characterization of American research on political representation concerns the period when the rational actor approach has dominated the scene (Mayhew 1974; Fiorina 1977; Fenno 1978; Cain et al. 1987; cf. Sinclair 1983). The initial study in the field was of course focused on policy representation (cf. Eulau and Karps 1977). Moreover, the internal British debate on political representation has largely centred on service responsiveness in the form of case work performed by MPs (Searing 1985).

[5] A conclusion reached was that the electoral system is not a fundamental cause of variations in MPs' focus of representation (Bogdanor 1984: 299). It should be added that the study in question also characterized MP–constituency linkages as generally weak. However, the criteria used for reaching this conclusion are unclear to me. My reading of the individual-country chapters is that Western representatives keep contact with their constituents in a multitude of ways. A possible explanation to the surprising conclusion would be that in the end the argumentation falls back on the European tradition of paying most attention to policy representation and ignoring other aspects of responsiveness.

However, the fact that the local approach might be the most valid with regards to non-policy aspects of political representation does not mean that the same is true with *policy representation*. On this matter, which many would argue concerns the single most important aspect of political representation, we have little hard empirical evidence for assessing the relative validity of the two approaches. From the European perspective the idea that there is a local policy linkage between constituents and their specific representatives has been viewed as so far-fetched that it has seldom been tested empirically.[6] Both approaches have been applied to the case of the USA, but rarely in a manner that explicitly compares the relative strength of local and national policy linkages between voters and their representatives.

The analysis in this chapter will begin to fill this apparent gap in our understanding of policy representation in Western democracies. The local approach is given a fair chance to prove its general validity; the analysis will tell us whether European political scientists have been overlooking a relevant policy linkage between voters and their representatives. Moreover, it will also give us an estimate of the relative strength of the two approaches in the US political setting.

LOGIC OF THE ANALYSIS

The strongest argument against the validity of the local approach is that parliamentary parties are usually tightly disciplined when voting on policy matters. If we take representatives' roll-call behaviour as the dependent variable, there is only marginal within-party variation to explain (Thomassen 1991). However, to concentrate on the final vote rather than on the policy views of representatives is to take a static approach toward the policy-making process. Western political parties are not only homogeneous actors; they are also arenas for debates and internal struggles over policy proposals. Decisions on large policy matters that face the nation are likely to be preceded by more or less fierce internal debates. Constituents who are in close agreement with their representatives on policy matters are likely to have someone championing their views in these debates. Or to present these ideas in another context, it seems reasonable to argue that it can make a difference whether a radical Social Democratic constituency is represented by radical, centrist, or conservative Social Democrats.

---

[6] The one exception, albeit not a minor one, is Converse and Pierce's study on France (1986).

According to this way of looking at political representation, two premises must be fulfilled if local policy linkages are to exist between constituents and their specific representatives. First, there must be geographical variations in policy views within parties; and second, these variations must be picked up by the representatives who are tied to the territorial areas in question.

This study looks into these premises by analysing the data in three steps. First, we test for territorially anchored variations in policy views of voters and representatives by means of a series of one-way analysis of variance, with area of residence as the independent variable. Second, we look further into the prerequisites for local policy linkages by testing for the existence of an independent local dynamic in policy views of voters and representatives. Certain local regularities in policy views—for instance, that both socialist and conservative voters of a particular constituency are relatively radical in comparison with other socialists and conservatives—would indicate that the process of opinion formation is at least partly driven by local forces. That in turn would make it more likely that representatives have an independent relationship with their constituents over and above the national linkage.

The third and final step of the analysis is to test directly for whether constituents are better represented by their specific representatives than by the collective of representatives. By 'better represented' we mean that there is a closer agreement in policy views between constituents and those they represent. This final analysis can be viewed as a test for the existence of independent local policy linkages over and above national, collective linkages.

It should be noted that this analysis differs from Weissberg's (1978) test for the degree of collective and dyadic policy representation. In reanalysing data from the Miller and Stokes representation study of 1958, Weissberg compared the level of policy agreement between constituents and their representatives (dyadic representation) with the level of policy agreement between the electorate as a whole and all representatives (collective representation). He found that voters were better represented collectively than dyadically in the sense that the difference between all representatives and all districts in the aggregate was smaller than the average difference between member of Congress and constituents on the dyadic basis. In contrast, this analysis compares, on the one hand, the levels of agreement between local constituents and their specific representatives, and on the other hand, between local constituents and the collective of representatives.

Thus, in concrete terms, Weissberg showed that the electorate as a whole were in closer agreement with the collective of representatives than voters of a particular constituency were with their own representatives. The present analysis will tell whether party voters of a particular constituency are in closer agreement with their own representatives than with the collective of party representatives. If they are we will conclude that there is an independent local policy linkage between constituents and their representatives.

Over the years the scholarly debate has made it painfully clear that empirical analyses of policy representation involve so many theoretical and practical decisons that no single analytical measurement can possibly cover all relevant aspects of the topic (Achen 1978). To repeat it yet again, the question posed here is whether the opinions of voters in different constituencies are more similar to those of the representatives from the same constituencies than they are to the position of the collective of representatives. A legitimate alternative question to pose is whether representatives respond to local variations in constituents' opinions: if mass scores are higher in some regions than in others, are the elite scores also higher in the same regions? The latter question, of course, is the one posed in the studies by Miller and Stokes (1963) and by Converse and Pierce (1986).[7]

I have opted for the former question mainly because it gives us an opportunity to compare the relative strength of local and national linkages between constituents and their representatives. When the strength of the local relationship is estimated in terms of representatives' responsiveness to local variations in constituents' policy views—as is the case in the traditional correlational studies of policy representation—it is not possible to compute a corresponding statistic for the responsiveness of the collective of representatives. Moreover, from the perspective of constituents, it seems highly relevant to find out whether their specific representatives hold policy views that are as close to their own as could be expected given the position of the collective of representatives.

DEFINING RELEVANT TERRITORIAL UNITS

As hinted above, the two approaches to political representation presuppose that there are different causal processes at work. According to the party-collectivistic approach, policy representation is a nationalized affair. Voters and representatives all over the country take their cues from the same debates. In contrast, according to the local approach policy representation is a matter between voters of a particular territorial unit and their specific representatives. Both voters and representatives are affected by sub-national factors. Thus, if the local approach is to be competitive, opinions must be shaped to a degree by local forces. If there are no local opinion formation processes, then there

---

[7] This distinction was pointed out to me by Roy Pierce.

are no independent local opinions. In the absence of local opinions, there are no local sentiments for representatives to recognize.

A necessary step in an empirical evaluation of the two approaches to policy representation is to define relevant sub-national territorial units. If electoral control were the only factor to consider, the task would be easy. We could start immediately to collect data at the level of official electoral districts. However, such a view would be unhappily formalistic. This is so because even in PR systems it is the rule rather than the exception that votes cast have formal bearing only on which persons will represent a particular territorial unit, and not on the national outcome of the election. Thus, to look solely at territorial units that are acknowledged in the electoral law would preclude by definition collective representation on a national basis, not only in the USA and other polities that practise single-member district voting systems, but in most multi-member district systems as well.

Rather than relying on a formal definition, we will look for local policy linkages in territorial units that are functionally relevant in the sense that there might be an independent opinion formation process going on. The concept of local opinion formation should be broadly defined. It should include long-term factors, such as historical experiences that have shaped moral and cultural values, as well as short-term factors, such as politicians who capitalize on events like the closure of a major factory.

Functionally relevant geographical constituencies could be defined by boundaries for the nomination process, but they could also be defined by, for example, local media markets, boundaries for party organizations, or borders of traditional cultural values. Or, to express this reasoning in a direct way: given the opinion formation processes at work, it might be more relevant for our understanding of local policy representation to study whether southern Democrats are in agreement with Democratic members of Congress from the south than it is to study whether the constituents of the third district of Arkansas are in agreement with their particular representative. Which of these two levels that is the more relevant is context bound; indeed, relevance may vary from issue area to issue area.

In this study a wide net is cast. We will look for local policy linkages at two different levels, both regionally and locally. The rationale for this conceptualization is that the two levels may reflect different prerequisites for political opinion formation. The regional level mainly reflects traditional differences in political orientations among the voting public. The local level reflects organizational aspects of politics, particularly the operations of political parties.

In this study, regions are defined as follows: in France we make use of the nine regions specified by Converse and Pierce (1986: 170–1) to be distinct and relatively homogeneous in terms of left–right orientations. In Sweden we select eight regions known to show homogeneous voting patterns among citizens (Oskarson 1994). The West German regions are identical to the ten *Länder* that were officially represented in the Bundestag, which means that each region is an independent factor in German politics. In the USA, the fifty states have been clustered into seven regions that we believe capture traditional differences in values and voting patterns.[8]

At the local level, we have for the Swedish case followed the twenty-eight official electoral districts, which are major focal points for the organization of parties. In the USA we follow the boundaries for the fifty states, which all have independent party organizations. In West Germany the local level is defined by boundaries for thirty-one official *Regierungsbezirken*. These geographical units have no immediate meaning for party organizations, but they are politically relevant in that citizens tend to identify with the unit in question. No local level has been defined for France.

As in previous chapters, this analysis pertains to the legislative body that is closest to the electorate for each respective country: the French National Assembly, the West German Bundestag, the US House of Representatives, and the Swedish Riksdag (the Second Chamber in 1968).

In conducting this analysis we have obviously taken far-reaching liberties with the US political system. In a way we are trying to estimate what local policy representation would look like if representatives were elected in multi-member districts on a statewide or regional basis, much as many parliamentary democracies function. This is done partly to get more reliable estimates of constituents' policy views, as well as to enhance cross-country comparisons. The main reason, however, is theoretical. If we adopt a non-formalistic view of political representation, we should search for local policy linkages on geographical levels that are relevant for opinion formation processes. Critics who nevertheless find the exercise purely artificial may take comfort in that we close the chapter with a repeat of the analysis in a setting faithful to US electoral laws.

To make the results comprehensible we will report only data pertaining to the two largest parties in each country; that is, a party of the left and a party

[8] The seven US regions are as follows: *North-East*: Maine; New Hampshire; Vermont; Connecticut; New York; New Jersey; *Atlantic Coast*: Virginia; North Carolina; West Virginia; Florida; Maryland; *Midwest*: Minnesota; Iowa; Illinois; Michigan; Wisconsin; Ohio; Indiana; Missouri; Nebraska; *South*: Alabama; Georgia; Louisiana; Mississippi; South Carolina; Tennessee; Kentucky; *South-West*: Texas; New Mexico; Arkansas; Arizona; Oklahoma; *Rocky Mountain*: Colorado; Utah; Kansas; Idaho; Montana; Wyoming; North Dakota; South Dakota; *West*: California; Oregon; Washington; Hawaii; Alaska; Nevada.

of the right.[9] The data used are by now familiar. Policy views of constituents and representatives will be measured as in previous chapters in this volume. That means that we have a measure of summary ideological self-placements in all four countries. Measurements of specific policy views were obtained from a varying number of questions included in respective studies: twenty in the Swedish studies of 1968 and 1985; eleven in the West German study of 1988; seven in the French study of 1967; and seven in the US study of 1987.[10]

A complicating factor in this analysis is the grim fact that good survey research is costly. Since we use national samples of voters to study local representation, we are bound to end up with somewhat unreliable measures of constituents' policy views at the constituency level. The smallest average sample sizes in this comparative study are 65 and 61 respectively (for West Germany and the USA, both on the local level).[11] This is certainly not ideal, but these problems are no more pressing than is normal in this kind of analysis.

GEOGRAPHICAL VARIATIONS IN POLICY VIEWS

A necessary condition for the existence of independent local policy linkages is that voters' policy views must vary between the relevant geographical areas; if districts are in high agreement there is not much variation for local representatives to identify. In their study on political representation in France, Converse and Pierce (1986: 511–20) lay out the full logic of the argument. For this analysis the bottom line is that we need to know whether voters' opinions are distributed in such a way that between-district variation is substantial in relation to within-district variation.[12]

With the problem phrased in this way, the choice of statistical measurement is obvious. As described by Converse and Pierce, the standard technique to estimate variation among districts is to compute the eta-measure,

---

[9] This information is of course only relevant for the European countries. For Sweden the two parties are 'Social Democrats' and 'Moderates'; for West Germany they are 'Social Democrats' and 'Christian Democrats' (including CSU); and for France they are 'The Left Party Family' (Socialists and Communists combined) and 'Gaullists'. Other way of coding parties gives essentially the same results.

[10] For the French case both winning and losing candidates are included. As regards estimates of public opinion among US constituents we rely mainly on the 1986 ANES House Election Study. However, for ideological orientations on the local (state) level we rely on the 1988 Senate Study.

[11] For the US case, this figure is based on the thirty-two states that are present in the 1986 House Study.

[12] Although it is a question of theoretical importance, we will not take into consideration here the absolute sum of variation between districts.

which is the ratio of the between-district variance to the total observed variance. The statistic can be interpreted in a simple way: the higher the eta-value the greater the relative variation between districts, and hence the higher the potential for local policy linkages.

This analysis follows the traditional path by computing the eta-value for ideological self-placements and for views on specific policy issues, with area of residence as an independent variable. In accordance with the analytical framework, the eta-value is computed for both regional and local geographical areas in the four countries. In comparison to the Converse and Pierce study, which concentrates on the overall variations at the voter level, two additional pieces of information are reported. First, we investigate whether geographical differences are present within political parties. If there are to be unique local policy linkages between voters and their respective representatives, there must be additional variations in policy views for representatives to identify once the national forces of parties have been at work. Furthermore, there is no reason for the analysis to be restricted to the voter level. The logic applies for representatives as well. For example, if party discipline is so strong that representatives' policy views are perfectly homogeneous, we may stop searching for independent local policy linkages no matter how territorially differentiated voters may be.

On the basis of previous research, we can formulate four expectations for the outcome of the analysis. First, since political conflicts are not regularly territorially anchored, and since it is even more rare that intra-party differences follow territorial boundaries, we expect territorial differentiation of policy views to be moderately high at most. In summarizing their findings along with results from previous studies, even such proponents of the local approach as Converse and Pierce concluded that within-district variation is generally considerably higher than between-district variation. But, they add, 'between district variation can nonetheless be counted on to be much less than trivial' (Converse and Pierce 1986: 517).

Second, since US parties are known to be much less cohesive than the parties of parliamentary systems, we expect US parties to have the highest eta-values. We also expect that federal systems, such as those of the USA and West Germany, are more likely than unitary France and Sweden to show geographical variations in policy views of voters and representatives. Third, given the uniting force of political parties, we expect eta-values to be lower and less likely to be statistically significant within parties than they are for geographical areas taken as a whole. Fourth, since party-discipline is mainly an elite phenomenon, we expect territorial differentiation and hence eta-values to be lower and less likely to be statistically significant among representatives than among voters.

Peter Esaiasson

TABLE 6.1. Geographical variations in ideological orientation among constituents and representatives (eta-values)

(*a*) Regional level

	Constituents			Representatives		
	All	Left	Right	All	Left	Right
France	0.19[a]	0.19[a]	0.11	0.15	0.16	0.45
Sweden	0.14[a]	0.00	0.14	0.19	0.39	0.63
USA	0.08	0.15[a]	0.08	0.48[a]	0.54[a]	0.68[a]
West Germany	0.22[a]	0.39[a]	0.30[a]	0.14	0.24	0.22

(*b*) Local level

	Constituents			Representatives		
	All	Left	Right	All	Left	Right
Sweden	0.17[a]	0.17	0.22	0.14	0.23	0.42[a]
USA	0.21[a]	0.27[a]	0.21	0.67[a]	0.71	0.83[a]
West Germany	0.28[a]	0.36[a]	0.39[a]	0.26	0.37	0.52

[a] $p \leq 0.10$

Note: Entries are eta-values resulting from a one-way analysis of variance with geographical residence as independent variable and ideological self-placements as the dependent variable.

The results in Table 6.1, which shows the eta-values for ideological self-placement in the four countries, only partly confirm the expectations. The first expectation—that geographical differentiations are moderately high at most—gets rather clear support. In their study Converse and Pierce (1986: 517) employed a standard for what to expect when they concluded that values of eta are 'extremely common in the .28–.30 range'. If we accept that comparisons of absolue eta-values are meaningful, the etas reported in Table 6.1 reach this standard in only about 40 per cent of the cases. Moreover, more often than not the coefficients fail to reach even such a moderate level for statistical significance as 0.10 (F-tests).

The second expectation—that geographical differentiation is higher in federal systems than in unitary systems, and particularly high in the USA —receives less support. True, the highest eta-values for ideological self-placements are found among US representatives and among West German voters and representatives. US voters are less geographically divided, but as we shall see this is partly a consequence of their being generally less ideologically constrained than their European counterparts (cf. Thomassen in this volume). However, in most cases the differences are minor indeed. The strongest impression from the results displayed in Table 6.1 is one of internation similarities, not one of individual country differences.

The two remaining expectations—that eta-values should be relatively low within parties and among representatives—are not at all fulfilled. Quite unexpectedly, etas are even higher among representatives than among voters, and higher within parties than in geographical areas taken as a whole. That is, even though parties and representatives are relatively homogeneous groups, the remaining variation in ideological self-placements is distributed in such a way that between-district variation is substantial. Thus national forces of opinion formation are strong but not completely dominant, and those forces work just as efficiently among voters as among representatives. Also, since territorial differentiation is relatively high among elected representatives it appears as if party discipline relates more to the final act of voting in parliament than to the personal views of representatives; strong party leaders are able to force rank-and-file representatives to vote cohesively, not necessarily to make them think unanimously.

Tables 6.2 and 6.3 give the corresponding information for views on specific policy issues in the four countries. To enhance presentation, results are shown in a highly condensed form. Table entries indicate the average eta-value over all policy issues (Table 6.2) and the proportion of eta-values that are statistically significant on the 0.10-level (Table 6.3). The latter information is presented as a corrective to conclusions based solely on the size of the eta-coefficient; in this kind of analysis degrees of freedom will always be smaller in surveys of representatives than of constituents.

Eta-values for specific policy views turn out to be similar to those registered for ideological orientation. The only difference is among US voters, where between-district variations are somewhat higher and more likely to be statistically significant. Thus, the basic structure of the results still holds: between-district variations are limited but non-trivial; variations are only slightly higher in the USA and West Germany than in Sweden and France; between-district variations are somewhat higher within parties than within territories as wholes; and between-district variations are higher among representatives than among voters.

As mentioned in other chapters in this volume, the battery of specific policy issues included in the available data sets are not randomly selected. Most issues stand a good chance of being thoroughly nationalized (e.g. salient left–right issues, and international affairs). Thus, it may well be that our results underestimate real territorial differentiation in policy views. Since the Swedish surveys include a small number of specific issues that can be classified as relating to a cultural/moral dimension of politics, where there

TABLE 6.2. Geographical variations in views on specific policy issues among constituents and representatives: average eta-values disregarding the level of significance

(*a*) Regional level

	Constituents			Representatives			Number of issues
	All	Left	Right	All	Left	Right	
France	0.13	0.14	0.16	0.16	0.23	0.40	7
Sweden 1968	0.11	0.10	0.20	0.18	0.24	0.39	20
Sweden 1985	0.10	0.09	0.13	0.16	0.22	0.32	20
USA	0.14	0.20	0.14	0.35	0.40	0.51	7
West Germany	0.14	0.18	0.19	0.17	0.29	0.32	11

(*b*) Local level

	Constituents			Representatives			Number of issues
	All	Left	Right	All	Left	Right	
Sweden 1968	0.17	0.18	0.37	0.32	0.48	0.70	20
Sweden 1985	0.14	0.19	0.26	0.24	0.42	0.59	20
USA	0.23	0.30	0.28	0.61	0.69	0.85	7
West Germany	0.22	0.29	0.34	0.30	0.48	0.49	11

Note: Entries are a summary of a series of one-way analysis of variance with geographical residence as the independent variable and views on various specific policy issues as the dependent variables.

might be better opportunities for influence on local opinions, we can learn to what extent our findings are dependent on the actual samples of issues.

A closer investigation of the Swedish data shows that the degree of territorial differentiation in policy views among voters and representatives is quite similar for moral/cultural issues and for other issues. When we separate issues relating to pornography, abortion, and defence spending from other issues, etas are on the average only slightly higher than for the total sample of issues.[13] Thus, at least for the issues salient enough to be included in the available surveys, the content of the issues seems to be less consequential.

Taken together these results form an important conclusion for the remainder of this study: the national forces of parties and party discipline are strong, but they do not take away the potential for local policy representation, not

---

[13] The same is true for the items on abortion that were included in the US and West German studies.

TABLE 6.3. Geographical variations in views on specific policy issues among constituents and representatives: proportion of issues for which differences between geographical areas are statistically significant (%)

(*a*) Regional level

	Constituents			Representatives			Number of issues
	All	Left	Right	All	Left	Right	
France	71	29	29	14	29	0	7
Sweden 1968	90	50	35	10	30	5	20
Sweden 1985	80	25	25	10	15	30	20
USA	100	100	71	57	57	57	7
West Germany	100	54	54	18	45	18	11

(*b*) Local level

	Constituents			Representatives			Number of issues
	All	Left	Right	All	Left	Right	
Sweden 1968	85	65	35	5	20	5	20
Sweden 1985	75	55	40	0	5	30	20
USA	100	100	57	57	29	29	7
West Germany	100	91	91	9	36	27	11

Note: Entries are a summary of a series of one-way analysis of variance with geographical residence as the independent variable and views on various specific policy issues as the dependent variables. The boundary for statistically significant relationships has been set to $p \leq 0.10$.

even for salient left–right issues. If representatives are able to pick up the existing territorial differentiations among voters there will be independent local policy linkages for most types of issues.

TERRITORIAL DYNAMICS

To further scrutinize the argument suggested by proponents of the local approach, we need to learn more about the processes that created the observed territorial differentiations. It is a necessary condition for the validity of the local approach that constituents' opinions are shaped to a degree by local forces. If the opinions of constituents are completely determined by national forces, then the policy relationship between constituents and their designated representatives is a mere formality, regardless of the size of registered correlation coefficients.

To sort out in detail a possible local component in the process of opinion formation is of course an immensely complicated task. However, Miller and Särlvik (1975) have argued that we can travel part of the way by searching for observable consequences of local forces. Their idea was to look at the relationship between parties on the local (sub-national) level. If opinions of constituents are affected by local forces it is likely that policy views of left partyists and right partyists in a particular constituency are somehow inter-related. Should the policy views of left partyists and right partyists be inde-pendent of each other on the local level, then it is less plausible, although not logically impossible, that local forces are of general importance when opin-ions are shaped.

Specifically, if there is a local component to the process of opinion forma-tion, then we would probably observe one of two patterns: local polities would be either *polarized* or *unified*. In a polarized local polity, constituents and/or representatives belong to different ideological camps within their respective party; that is, if left partyists in a particular constituency are more radical than left partyists in other constituencies, right partyists in the same constituency also tend to be more conservative than right partyists in other constituencies. Correspondingly, in a unified local polity, constituents and representatives belong to the same ideological camp within their respective party; that is, both left partyists and right partyists in a particular constituency tend to be radicals (or conservatives, or centrists). An intriguing quality of this analytical approach is that it allows the process of opinion formation to work differently for constituents and representatives. For example, it is fully possible that local polities tend to be unified among constituents and polar-ized among representatives.

As pointed out by Miller and Särlvik (1975), rank correlations (Spearman's Rho) are a useful statistical diagnostic for the existence of this kind of local dynamics in policy views. Positive rank correlations indicate unified local polities, whereas negative rank correlations indicate polarized local polities. Following their suggestion, Table 6.4 shows rank correlations between left partyists and right partyists for ideological self-placement in the four countries.

This time the results are less favourable for proponents of the local approach to political representation. Even if we set a non-conservative standard for statistical significance, it is only in three of fourteen possible cases that the rank correlation coefficient reaches the critical region: among US voters and representatives on the local level, and among Swedish repres-entatives on the regional level. In the US case local polities are unified, whereas among Swedish representatives local polities are polarized.

Based on this analysis the conclusion would be that local forces are mainly, and perhaps only, important in the formation of US opinion. However,

TABLE 6.4. Geographical dynamics in ideological orientations of constituents and representatives: rank correlations between left partyists and right partyists (Spearman's Rho)

(*a*) Regional level

	Constituents left party/right party	Representatives left party/right party	Number of units
France	$+0.37^{.33}$	$+0.24^{.53}$	9
Sweden	$-0.22^{.61}$	$-0.76^{.03}$	8
USA	$-0.31^{.50}$	$+0.52^{.23}$	7
West Germany	$-0.15^{.68}$	$-0.28^{.42}$	10

(*b*) Local level

	Constituents left party/right party	Representatives left party/right party	Number of units
Sweden	$-0.17^{.29}$	$-0.18^{.38}$	28
USA	$+0.41^{.00}$	$+0.39^{.12}$	50 (17)
West Germany	$-0.15^{.43}$	$+0.08^{.69}$	31

Note: Entries are rank correlations of mean ideological self-placements of left partyists and right partyists. The statistic is computed for both regional units and local units. For local-level US representatives the statistic is based on only 17 states for which we have information on both Democrats (left party) and Republicans (right party). Probabilities are two-tailed tests.

territorial dynamics are more present when attention is turned to specific policy issues. From Table 6.5, which shows the proportion of specific policy issues for which rank correlations are statistically significant, it is clear that local parties are interrelated in several issues in all four countries. Thus, there seems to be a local component to the process of opinion formation for a considerable number of policy issues. Only in Sweden in 1985 do almost all issues show the expected pattern if opinion formation is predominantly nationalized —that is, no relationship between parties on any sub-national level.

The highest proportion of issues (over 40 per cent) showing sub-national relationships between parties is found among West German voters (local level) and US voters (regional level). But among French voters (regional level), Swedish voters in 1968 (regional level), and US representatives (regional level), one-fourth of the issues show a relationship between parties. In sum, the findings correspond well with our initial expectations on territorial differentations in policy views: local dynamics are stronger than trivial; local dynamics are somewhat stronger in federal systems than in unitary systems; and local dynamics are stronger among constituents than among representatives.

TABLE 6.5. Geographical dynamics in positions on specific policy issues: proportion of issues for which rank correlations between left partyists and right partyists are statistically significant (%)

(*a*) Regional level

	Constituents left party/right party	Representatives left party/right party	Number of issues	Number of units
France	29	14	7	9
Sweden 1968	25	16	20	8
Sweden 1985	5	7	20	8
USA	43	0	7	7
W. Germany	27	9	11	10

(*b*) Local level

	Constituents left party/right party	Representatives left party/right party	Number of issues	Number of units
Sweden 1968	10	10	20	28
Sweden 1985	0	0	20	28
USA	29	29	7	50 (17)
W. Germany	45	18	11	31

Note: Entries are a summary of series of rank correlation analysis (Spearman's Rho). The boundary for statistically significant relationships has been set to $p \leq 0.10$.

Table 6.6 gives the complementary information on the direction of the relationships. Table entries are the proportion of specific policy issues for which the rank correlation coefficient is positive, disregarding the level of statistical significance. High percentages indicate that local polities tend to be unified (most coefficients are positive), whereas low percentages indicate that local polities tend to be polarized (most coefficients are negative).

The results of voters can be easily summarized. In all four countries and on both the regional and local levels, positive rank correlations are more common than negative rank correlations. Although only two of the individual distributions clearly differ from what could be expected by chance, there is on the whole a strong tendency for local politics to be unified. Most often left party voters and right party voters in a particular constituency belong to the same ideological camp within their respective party. Differences in policy views are of course not eliminated, but it appears that local forces do shape supporters' opinions.

For representatives the results are mixed. Like their constituents, US representatives are positively interrelated in their local polities. That is, conservative Republicans tend to go together with conservative Democrats, and radical Democrats tend to go together with radical Republicans. West

TABLE 6.6. Geographical dynamics in views on on specific policy issues: proportion of positive relationships between left partyists and right partyists (%)

(*a*) Regional level

	Constituents left party/right party	Representatives left party/right party	Number of issues	Number of units
France	86	29	7	9
Sweden 1968	60	32	20	8
Sweden 1985	60	61	20	8
USA	86	100[a]	7	7
W. Germany	64	55	11	10

(*b*) Local level

	Constituents left party/right party	Representatives left party/right party	Number of issues	Number of units
Sweden 1968	85[a]	35	20	28
Sweden 1985	65	61	20	28
USA	71	86	7	50
W. Germany	91[a]	64	11	31

Note: Entries are a summary of a series of rank correlation analysis (Spearman's Rho). A dominance of positive relationships indicates *relative unity* between left partyists and right partyists, whereas a dominance of negative relationships (i.e. a low proportion of positive relationships) indicates *relative polarization* between left partyists and right partyists.

[a] The probability that this distribution would appear if the underlying process was random is less than 10 per cent.

German representatives are also more often than not unified on the sub-national level. French and Swedish representatives, however, show a tendency to be polarized in their local polities. Thus, in France and Sweden the opinion formation processes differ between representatives and constituents. The pattern observed among representatives is what would be expected if representatives were mainly concerned with competing electorally by staking out positions opposite those of their competitors. The observed tendencies are empirically weak, but they nevertheless support the idea that the relationship between US constituents and representatives may differ from that of the parliamentary systems of Europe.

LOCAL POLICY LINKAGES

By now we know that the potential for independent local policy linkages exists. Policy views of voters and representatives differ between territorial units, and there is evidence of a local component to the process of opinion formation.

The potential may be somewhat higher in federal systems than in unitary systems, and somewhat higher in weak party systems than in strong party systems. However, in all four countries under scrutiny it is fully possible that independent local policy linkages between constituents and their specific representatives are developed. What remains to be discovered is whether representative systems pick up the observed territorial differences.

In this study, an independent local policy linkage is said to exist where there is higher policy congruence between the policy views of constituents and their specific representatives than there is between constituents and the collective of representatives. From this definition we can choose a straight-forward analytical technique. The first step involves computing the mean position on various policy issues of the following: voters of a particular con-stituency, representatives of this particular constituency, and the collective of representatives. This computation is repeated for every unit in question.[14] In the next step we compute the average district-by-district difference between constituents and their specific representatives disregarding the sign of the dif-ference. Thereafter we compute the same statistic for the difference between constituents and the collective of representatives. Finally, the two summary statistics are compared.

The crucial information is found in the sum of the final comparison between the two summary statistics. When the sum is positive, constituents are on average in higher agreement with their specific representatives than with the collective of representatives. In this case an independent local pol-icy linkage is said to exist. When the sum is negative, constituents are in higher agreement with the collective of representatives than with their specific rep-resentatives and there is no independent local policy linkage. Table 6.7 shows the results for ideological orientations in the four countries.

For proponents of the local approach to policy representation, the outcome of this basic empirical test is problematic. There is only a single case where constituents are significantly closer to their specific representatives than to the collective of representatives (among West German right partyists on the local level). In three more cases local constituents are slightly closer to their specific representatives. The remaining seventeen cases show the opposite relationship—that constituents are in higher agreement with the collective of representatives than with their designated representatives (although only two of the differences are significant at the 0.10 level). Thus, there is very little evidence of independent local policy linkages in any of the four countries.[15]

---

[14] As defined in this study the mean position of the collective of representatives is of course a constant.

[15] The probability that 17 of 21 cases should be either positive or negative if the under-lying process was random is less than 5 per cent.

TABLE 6.7. Local policy linkages: agreement in ideological orientations between constituents and representatives (means and difference of means)

(*a*) Regional level

	All Mean difference between constituents and representatives			Left party Mean difference between constituents and representatives			Right party Mean difference between constituents and representatives		
	Part vs part	Part vs whole	diff.	Part vs part	Part vs whole	diff.	Part vs part	Part vs whole	diff.
France	18.4	17.6	$-0.80^{.54}$	19.3	19.2	$-0.01^{.99}$	16.6	15.2	$-1.40^{.52}$
Sweden	0.62	0.52	$-0.10^{.51}$	0.69	0.70	$+0.01^{.89}$	0.35	0.53	$-0.18^{.36}$
USA	0.64	0.23	$-0.41^{.07}$	0.79	0.84	$+0.05^{.81}$	0.87	0.77	$-0.10^{.67}$
W. Germany	0.77	0.90	$-0.13^{.20}$	1.00	0.97	$-0.03^{.80}$	1.05	1.27	$+0.22^{.12}$

(*b*) Local level

	All Mean difference between constituents and representatives			Left party Mean difference between constituents and representatives			Right party Mean difference between constituents and representatives		
	Part vs part	Part vs whole	diff.	Part vs part	Part vs whole	diff.	Part vs part	Part vs whole	diff.
Sweden	0.66	0.58	$-0.08^{.35}$	0.76	0.73	$-0.03^{.66}$	0.60	0.41	$-0.19^{.10}$
USA	0.72	0.43	$-0.29^{.11}$	0.89	0.83	$-0.06^{.56}$	0.72	0.43	$-0.29^{.11}$
W. Germany	0.92	0.89	$-0.03^{.70}$	1.26	1.09	$-0.16^{.15}$	0.90	1.29	$+0.39^{.00}$

Note: Negative differences indicate that local constituents are in better agreement with the collective of representatives ('whole') than they are with their specific representatives ('part'). Probabilities are t-tests, two-tailed.

The results are even more unambiguous regarding specific policy views. Despite the fact that territorial differentiations may be somewhat larger for specific policy views than for ideological orientations, it is extremely rare to find evidence of an independent policy linkage. Indeed, in only one case of a total of 363 observations are constituents in significantly closer agreement with their specific representatives than with the collective of representatives (details not shown).[16] The opposite relationship—that constituents are

[16] The number of observations are calculated as follows: we have compared the dyadic to the collective relationship in four countries on two geographical levels among a left party, a right party, and among the totality in 7 to 20 specific policy issues.

significantly closer to the collective of representatives than to their specific representatives—is much more common. On the local level more than one-third of the issues in all four countries show this pattern, the USA included.

It is worth emphasizing that this finding is not a statistical artefact. Weissberg's (1978) study of the relative strength of collective as opposed to dyadic representation in the US House of Representatives has been criticized for being mathematically tautological. Given his mathematical definitions of dyadic and collective representation, Weissberg's empirical test cannot fail to confirm that voters are better represented collectively than dyadically (Hurley 1982: 121). That kind of critique does not apply to this analysis. For instance, the relationship among West German right partyists provides evidence that it is fully feasible for representatives to pick up territorial differentiations in policy views of constituents. However, a similar critique that needs to be addressed is that the total variations in policy views are so limited that differences are not very likely to be statistically significant; local representatives may tend to be closer to their specific constituents than to the collective of representatives, but only slightly so. To test for this possibility we have calculated the proportion of specific policy issues for which con-stituents are in higher agreement with their specific representatives, disregarding the level of statistical significance.

As the results in Table 6.8 indicate, this is not generally the case. In 21 of 24 instances a majority of the specific policy issues shows the opposite rela-tionship, with constituents being closer to the collective of representatives. Although only about one-half of the individual distributions are statistically different from what could be expected by chance, the overall pattern is clear.[17] With regards to policy representation, 'normality' can be defined as a situ-ation in which voters of a particular constituency are somewhat to markedly closer to the collective of representatives then they are to their specific representatives. Only rarely is there evidence of an independent local policy linkage, i.e. that constituents are closer to their specific representatives than they are to the collective of representatives.

Given the turns of the scholarly debate, the most surprising aspect of these findings is that the US case does not in any way differ from those of the other countries. There is as little evidence of independent local policy linkages in the USA as there is in unitary Sweden with its strong party system. Although the potential for local policy linkages may be higher in the USA than in other countries, the structure of the representational process turns out to be uni-versal: representatives rarely pick up territorial differentiations in policy views of voters.

---

[17] The probability that 21 of 24 cases should be negative if the underlying relationship was random is less than 5 per cent.

TABLE 6.8. Local policy linkages: proportion of specific policy issues in which constituents are in better agreement with the collective of representatives ('Whole') than they are with their local representatives ('Parts')

(*a*) Regional level

	All	Left party	Right party	Number of issues	Number of units
France	57	71	57	7	9
Sweden 1968	75[a]	65	80[a]	20	8
Sweden 1985	70	75[a]	70	20	8
USA	57	14	100[a]	7	7
W. Germany	64	73	36	11	10

(*b*) Local level

	All	Left party	Right party	Number of issues	Number of units
Sweden 1968	45	55	80[a]	20	28
Sweden 1985	90[a]	85[a]	75[a]	20	28
USA	100[a]	86	100[a]	7	50
W. Germany	82[a]	82[a]	91[a]	11	31

Note: Entries are a summary of a series of comparison between local representation (part vs. part) and collective representation (part vs. whole) on specific policy issues. High percentages indicate that constituents are in better agreement with the collective of representatives than they are with their local representatives on most issues.

[a] The probability that this distribution would appear if the underlying process was random is less than 10 per cent.

Sceptics may protest that the negative result is a consequence of the decision to take as units of analysis regions and states rather than formal electoral districts. Surely a test conducted in a setting true to the formalities of US politics would more positively validate the local approach to policy representation? Since both regions and states have shown territorial differentiations in policy views of constituents and representatives, I would argue that much of the sting of this criticism has been taken out, but it would nevertheless be of interest to perform the analysis on the level of electoral districts as well.

Luckily, we have the opportunity to go at least part of the way towards a proper empirical test of the proposition. In the US data set there is matching information on constituents and members of Congress for thirty-three districts (Smith et al. 1990; Herrera et al. 1992). By comparing the dyadic relationship between constituents and their specific representatives in these thirty-three districts to the relationship between the same constituents and the

TABLE 6.9. Local policy linkages in the USA: agreement in views on specific policy issues between constituents and representatives on the district level (means and difference of means)

	All Mean difference between policy views of constituents and representatives		
	Part vs part	Part vs whole	diff.
Defence	1.22	0.53	−0.69[.00]
Minority aid	1.74	0.92	−0.82[.00]
Central America	1.61	0.63	−0.98[.00]
Governmental service	1.77	0.71	−1.06[.00]
Standard of living	1.72	0.81	−0.91[.00]
Russia	1.48	0.89	−0.60[.00]
Abortion	1.22	1.18	−0.04[.80]

Note: Negative differences indicate that constituents are in better agreement with the collective of national representatives ('Whole') than they are with their local representative ('Part'). Only 33 districts with matching information on constituents and representatives are included.

collective of representatives, we can test whether the tendency of the results is altered when the analysis is performed in a setting truer to the formalities of the US system. Due to small sample sizes it is not meaningful to estimate constituents' opinions within parties. Hence the analysis does not take into consideration differences between parties or between winners and losers. Table 6.9 gives the results for the seven specific policy issues that were included in the US study.

This new analysis does not alter the basic findings. On the contrary, the results tell us that on a district basis US constituents on average are in much closer agreement with the collective of representatives than they are with their own specific representative. For six of the seven specific policy issues, differences are of substantial magnitude and are highly statistically significant. Of course, we cannot know what the outcome would be if we were able to look separately at Democrats and Republicans, or at winners and losers; it appears that the pattern of weak to non-existing local policy linkages does not depend on territorial differences.

CONCLUSIONS

The findings of this analysis suggest that there is little support for the notion of independent local policy linkages in the European setting, and it seems as if the party-collective approach is more relevant for the US case as well. Specifically, it is argued that in terms of policy views, voters of a particular constituency are generally in better agreement with the collective of party representatives than they are with their own specific representatives. This pattern is found in Sweden and West Germany as well as in France and the USA.

The reason that the party-collective approach to policy representation may be superior to the local approach for most electoral systems has to do with the forces that shape public opinion. To the extent that voters and representatives take their policy cues from national sources, there is little room for local policy linkages. In a nationalized representative system, voters of a particular region are electing one or more persons to be their representatives in the parliament; but in terms of policy views, the local connection between representatives and those who are represented is loose indeed.

Policy views of national figures have been considered important in the European context for a long time. It would appear that the process of opinion formation is increasingly nationalized in the USA as well. Of course, it would be highly interesting to use data from a time when US parties were less homogeneous than they are today to test the two approaches. From this perspective, a study of the US representational system of the 1970s may be very revealing.

While discussing consequences of the results presented here, it should be acknowledged that anyone who does not want to believe in the findings can easily justify that position. To mention a few possible methodological and theoretical objections, it can be argued that estimates of policy views of voters and representatives are unreliable; that the samples of policy issues included in the four studies are disadvantageous to the local approach (mostly national issues are covered); that the findings are based on arbitrarily defined territorial units; that the conceptual understanding of policy representation is questionable (it would have been more interesting to find out whether representatives respond to local variations in constituents' opinions than to test whether opinions of voters in different localities are absolutely similar to those of representatives from the same territories); and that the analytical procedure is flawed (computations should be based on medians rather than on means; on squared differences of means rather than on absolute differences; and representatives of a particular constituency should be excluded from the collective of representatives when distances are computed).[18]

There is no doubt that these and other objections are credible. Further studies in the field are clearly needed. Nevertheless I would argue that the local

---

[18] These are recommendations made in the literature (e.g. Huber and Powell 1994; Achen 1978), and by participants in the project.

approach to policy representation has been given a fair chance to prove its validity in comparison to the party-collective approach. If representatives really were maintaining a close policy relationship with their local constituents the results would have been different. The potential for local policy linkages is there; the problem is that various representational systems are not doing a good job identifying existing territorial differences. Local constituents are usually in closer policy agreement to the collective of representatives than they are to their representatives.

The findings do not in any way imply that the local approach to political representation is invalid. As discussed in the introduction, evidence indicates that Western representatives generally pay close attention to the interests of their constituents when providing personal services and securing public means. Furthermore, if we are concerned with formal electoral control, the local approach is by definition valid, and in many polities it is the *only* valid approach. However, when we analyse policy representation the basic finding of this study should be taken into account: once we know the policy views of the collective of party representatives, we gain very little empirical understanding of policy linkages by including in the analysis the views of specific representatives. In the process of policy representation, national forces are predominant.

Of course, European scholars in the field can react to the finding by shrugging their shoulders and saying 'I told you so.' What is surprising about the analysis is that the US experience appears so similar to the rest of the countries included in the study. Indeed, the empirical relevance of the geographical dimension to policy representation suggests that the political system does not matter all that much.

REFERENCES

Achen, Christopher (1978), 'Measuring Representation', *American Journal of Political Science*, 22: 475–510.

Bartels, Larry (1991), 'Constituency Opinion and Congressional Policy Making: The Reagan Defense Buildup', *American Political Science Review*, 85: 457–74.

Bogdanor, Vernon (ed.) (1984), *Representatives of the People: Parliamentarians and Constituents in Western Democracies* (London: Gower).

Cain, Bruce, Ferejohn, John, and Fiorina, Morris (1987), *The Personal Vote: Constituency Service and Electoral Independence* (Cambridge, Mass.: Harvard University Press).

Converse, Philip, and Pierce, Roy (1986), *Political Representation in France* (Cambridge, Mass.: Harvard University Press).

Esaiasson, Peter, and Holmberg, Sören (1996), *Representation from above: Members of Parliament and Representative Democracy in Sweden* (Aldershot: Dartmouth).

Eualu, Heinz, and Karps, Paul (1977), 'The Puzzle of Representation: Specifying Components of Responsiveness', *Legislative Studies Quarterly*, 2: 233–54.

Fenno, Richard (1978), *Home Style: House Members in Their District* (Boston: Little Brown).

Fiorina, Morris (1977), *Congress: Keystone of the Washington Establishment* (New Haven: Yale University Press).

Gallagher, Michael, and Marsh, Michael (eds.) (1988), *Candidate Selection in Comparative Perspective: The Secret Garden of Politics* (London: Sage).

Herrera, Cheryl, Herrera, Richard, and Smith, Eric R. A. N. (1992), 'Public Opinion and Congressional Representation', *Public Opinion Quarterly*, 56: 185–205.

Huber, John, and Powell, G. Bingham Jr. (1994), 'Congruence between Citizens and Policymakers in Two Visions of Liberal Democracy', *World Politics*, 46: 291–326.

Hurley, Patricia (1982), 'Collective Representation Reappraised', *Legislative Studies Quarterly*, 7: 119–36.

Kuklinski, James, and Segura, Gary M. (1995), 'Endogeneity, Exogeneity, Time, and Space in Political Representation', *Legislative Studies Quarterly*, 20: 3–21.

Lancaster, David, and Patterson, Thomas (1990), 'Comparative Pork Barrel Politics: Perceptions from the West German Bundestag', *Comparative Political Studies*, 22: 458–77.

Mayhew, David (1974), *Congress: The Electoral Connection* (New Haven: Yale University Press).

Miller, Warren, and Särlvik, Bo (1975), 'National vs. Constituency Representation in Sweden', Unpublished manuscript.

—— and Stokes, Donald (1963), 'Constituency Influence in Congress', *American Political Science Review*, 57: 45–56.

Oskarson, Maria (1994), *Klassröstning i Sverige: Rationalitet, lojalitet eller bara slentrian* (Stockholm: Nerenius & Santérus).

Page, Benjamin, and Shapiro, Robert (1992), *The Rational Public: Fifty Years of Trends in Americans' Policy Preferences* (Chicago: University of Chicago Press).

Patterson, Thomas (1991), *Does the Electoral Connection Extend to Europe? A Comparison of the Constituency Service Activities of Members of the West German Bundestag and the Danish Folketing* (Ann Arbor: UMI Dissertation Service).

Roth, Per-Anders (1996), *Riket, valkretsen och kommunen* (Göteborg: Statsvetenskapliga institutionen).

Searing, Donald (1985), 'The Role of the Good Constituency Member and the Practice of Representation in Great Britain', *Journal of Politics*, 47: 348–81.

Sinclair, Barbara (1983), 'Purposive Behavior in the US Congress: A Review Essay', *Legislative Studies Quarterly*, 8: 117–31.

Smith, Eric R. A. N., Herrera, Richard, and Herrera, Cheryl (1990), 'The Measurement Characteristics of Congressional Roll-Call Indexes', *Legislative Studies Quarterly*, 15: 283–95.

Stimson, James, MacKuen, Michael, and Erikson, Robert (1995), 'Dynamic Representation', *American Political Science Review*, 89: 543–65.

Taylor, Michelle (1992), 'Formal versus Informal Incentive Structures and Legislative Behavior: Evidence from Costa Rica', *Journal of Politics*, 54: 1055–73.

Thomassen, Jacques (1991), 'Empirical Research into Political Representation', in Hans-Dieter Klingemann, Richard Stöss, and Bernhard Wessels (eds.), *Politische Klasse und Politische Institutionen* (Opladen: Westdeutscher Verlag).

Uslaner, Erik (1985), 'Casework and Institutional Design: Reedeming Promises in the Promised Land', *Legislative Studies Quarterly*, 10: 35–52.

Weissberg, Robert (1978), 'Collective vs. Dyadic Representation in Congress', *American Political Science Review*, 72: 535–47.

Wlezien, Christopher (1996), 'Dynamics of Representation: The Case of US Spending on Defence', *British Journal of Political Science*, 26: 81–103.

7

System Characteristics Matter

Empirical Evidence from Ten Representation Studies

Bernhard Wessels

INTRODUCTION

Political representation lies at the heart of democratic systems. However, political representation is possible in political systems different from liberal democracies (Weissberg 1978: 547). But in no other system is representation as important in normative terms as in democracies. The normative theory of democracy explicitly calls for political representation. Dahl (1989: 95) regards as the reasonable justification for democracy that citizens are most effective in inducing government to do what they want by using orderly and peaceful means. However, representation is a complex phenomenon. It has been addressed from a variety of angles and dimensions and through different normative lenses. The smallest common denominator in normative terms, though, is that in a democracy there should be some match between the interests of the people and what representatives promote.

How this match can and/or should be reached is an open-ended debate in democratic theory. The mandate-independence controversy is most prominent in this respect (Pitkin 1967; Eulau 1978; Converse and Pierce 1986: ch. 16). Should representatives be controlled, and should electors be in a position to punish deserters, or should representatives act independently and according to their own judgement or personal conscience? It is not my intention here to enter this debate. The critical 'real-life problem of representation' was and is the 'responsibility of the governors to the governed' (Eulau 1978: 49). It is normatively assumed that representatives should serve the *interests*, if not the *will*, of those represented.

The research objective of this chapter is to investigate the impact of characteristics of political systems on policy representation. It is often asked how representation is affected by the two most central 'visions of liberal democracy', the 'majority-control vision' and the 'proportionate influence vision'

(Huber and Powell 1994). With respect to representatives one must consider the structure of electoral competition: who are the electors or the electoral units? Does a representative face a constituency where he has to gain a majority of votes, or is the position on a party list more important in becoming elected? Here the hypothesis is put forward that these two different mechanisms of electoral law affect the representatives' focus of representation and thereby the outcome of policy representation in a specific way: representatives in majoritarian systems should be more oriented towards the 'median voter,' whereas representatives in more proportional systems are more strongly oriented toward the representation of their party voters. With respect to voters the question is a mirror of that for MPs. What are the choices a voter can make? One can easily assume that the clearer the supply, the easier the choice that fits the voter's interest. The hypothesis investigated here suggests the more politically differentiated a party system is, the better off party voters are. These questions can only be answered by applying a comparative perspective. The advantage of this study is that it can make use of ten representation studies of five quite different democracies: France, Germany, the Netherlands, Sweden, and the United States of America.

In the following pages of this chapter, we first present our empirical approach, the data and measures being used. We then turn to a more detailed elaboration of our hypotheses on the relationship between characteristics of political systems and policy representation during the course of an empirical investigation which asks (*a*) to what degree electoral law puts particular demand on the focus of representation, thus influencing the mechanisms of policy representation, and (*b*) to what degree political supply structures of the party system have an impact on policy representation.

APPROACH, DATA, AND MEASUREMENTS

Research into political representation can be classified according to three aspects: (1) what are the representative units? (2) What are the dependent variables, i.e., how is representation measured in terms of content and in terms of methods? And (3) what are the explanatory variables?

One general distinction of *representative units* is whether they are collectivities or individuals. This is consistent with the distinction of collective and dyadic representation (Weissberg 1978). Units of collective representation in empirical research have been institutions like governments (Huber and Powell 1994), the legislature as a whole or parties in parliament (factions) (Farah 1980; Herrera et al. 1992; Holmberg 1989; Irwin and Thomassen 1975; Weissberg 1978; Wessels 1991), or parties (Dalton 1985; Porter 1995). Units of dyadic representation in empirical research have been legislators (Achen 1978; Barnes 1977, Converse and Pierce 1986; Farah 1980; Herrera et al. 1992; Jackson and King 1989; Miller and Stokes 1963).

The *dependent variables* vary across researches and measure different forms of representation. A general distinction can be made between outputs and positions. Collective outputs are decisions (such as votes/acts on laws, budgets, etc.), while individual outputs are votes (*decisional representation*, Holmberg 1989: 4). Positions can be measured in terms of mean policy position or ideological position of a collectivity or an individual (dyadic and collective *policy representation*). Cox (1997: 226) calls this *policy advocacy*.

Explanations of political representation have been searched for in the characteristics of the members of a collective representative body or in the individual legislator (socio-demographic characteristics, role orientations, electoral status/re-election chances) and to some extent in the information exchange between representatives and voters (newspaper reading, Converse and Pierce 1986; constituency contacts, Wessels 1991, 1993). Another body of possible explanations may exist in the characteristics of the system, whether those of the constituencies or those of political systems as a whole; but this has not received much attention due to a lack of comparative research on political representation. Only Dalton (1985), to a certain extent, and Huber and Powell (1994) very explicitly use system characteristics as explanatory variables of political representation. In opposing two pure system types — that of 'majority control' and the 'proportionate influence' type and a mixed category — Huber and Powell seek systemic explanations of the quality of representation or the degree of congruence in generalized policy positions (left–right position) between governments and electorates, by using variables measuring electoral competition, election outcomes, and legislative bargaining structure.

The *dependent variable* used here is a measure of the congruence in policy positions between representatives and represented, which is in line with many studies on political representation. This is only one aspect of representation. It is neither 'standing-for representation' (social representation) nor 'decisional representation' (acting-for representation) (Holmberg 1989: 4). But it is most likely that congruence in policy positions, i.e. *policy representation*, is a condition for decisional representation. A high degree of attitudinal congruence between leaders and voters evidently does not guarantee respective action on part of the representatives (Holmberg 1989). But with respect to representation in parliament this is not a counter-argument. In process terms, policy positions have to be present in parliament in the first place, in the sense that there are representatives supporting those positions, no matter whether they are able to influence political decisions (Wessels 1991: 330–4; Wessels

1993: 100–9). It could easily happen that the majority decides differently from the particular MP. But if a representative puts forward a position on agenda building, policy formation, bargaining, or decision-making in parliament that also matches that of his constituency or voters, he represents the policy positions of his constituency or voters. If there is congruence, then there is policy representation. Furthermore, research shows that there is a high correlation between attitudes and behaviour (Miller and Stokes 1963; Herrera et al. 1992; Sullivan and O'Connor, 1972).

In contrast to most studies on political representation, this study will use macro variables characterizing the electoral and the party systems to explain policy representation. With respect to the electoral system, we will use a measurement that characterizes the political systems on the majoritarian-proportional continuum and measures of the disproportionality of electoral systems. Programmatic differentiation and the number of parties will be considered for characterizing the party systems' measures of polarization.

The data used here were taken from a number of different representation studies, varying in the issues they looked at and also varying with respect to the time in which they were conducted. What they have in common is their general design as representation studies that measure policy orientations of the public and representatives in a comparable way. Since representation studies are an underdeveloped research area in most countries, and comparative efforts in this respect are still at their beginning, a secondary analysis of the few existing studies appears to be the only and best way for a comparative study of political representation. The studies used are Miller and Stokes's 'classic,' carried out in the United States in 1958, Converse and Pierce's study for France in 1967, Holmberg's, et al., studies for Sweden in 1968, 1985, and 1988, Thomassen's, et al., studies for the Netherlands in 1971, 1977, and 1989, Herrera's, et al., study for the USA in 1986–7, and Herzog and Wessels's study for Germany in 1988–9. Thus, a maximum of only four countries was examined at roughly similar points in time. However, since this chapter is an attempt to study *system differences* and their effect on policy representation, the time intervals between the studies present no serious challenge to the design. A more severe problem for comparison is that the studies deal with different numbers, contents, and scalings of policy issues. Even when bundled, these policy issues do not cover the same policy dimensions in all cases.

Given this heterogeneity, one nonetheless must make some assumptions and find a methodological solution to be able to draw comparisons. The first assumption is not exceedingly courageous though, assuming that all studies include issues that are of great importance in the respective polities at that particular point in time. The second is a 'structuralist' assumption. Since this chapter deals with the impact of structural characteristics of political systems on policy representation, it is assumed that on a general level one can abstract from the concrete content of the issues and concentrate on the structure of an overall policy-preference match.

Thus we will not look at single issues but rather at a composite measure of all issues under study, because mechanisms of representation could differ between issue domains. Miller and Stokes, for example, show in their study that different models of representation apply to different public issues (Miller and Stokes 1963). Since we deal with differences not *within* but *between* political systems, we can neglect this point here. Holmberg tentatively applies this strategy in his study in order to compare the Swedish results with results from the United States and France (Holmberg 1989: 13–15); we will follow the same procedure.

The measures used here are all based on the comparison of collectives. Collective measures compare collectivities of MPs with collectivities of voters. Two kinds of collective measures will be used: absolute and relative. While the absolute measure refers to *distance* (Achen 1978: 481), the relative measure refers to *responsiveness* (Achen 1978: 488). Absolute measures of congruence compare the absolute policy position of MPs with the absolute policy position of units of the electorate. In most cases this is a measure for differences in means. Relative measures compare the relative position of units of MPs with units of the electorate.

The absolute measure of distance used here is a standardized measure of absolute distances between representatives or groups of representatives and the electorate or voter groups. Since the range of issue scales differs between countries, all scales have been standardized to a minimum of 0 and a maximum of 100. From these scales *absolute differences* between the mean position of representatives or a group of representatives and the mean position of the electorate or groups of voters have been calculated, summed up, and divided by the number of issues included.[1] This is the *absolute distance measure*.

Two additional relative measures will be used. Since the main objective is to investigate the degree to which representatives in different systems are oriented toward policy representation of party voters as compared to the 'median

---

[1] The formula for standardizing the scales is: $x_{norm} = (x - 1) * (100/(max - 1))$ for scales with a minimum of 1; for scales with a minimum of 0 it is: $x_{norm} = x * 100/max$; where x is the original mean of a group on the policy scale and max the highest value of the scale. The formula for the absolute mean difference is: abs. mean diff. = sum of standardized absolute differences between representatives and represented across issues divided by the total number of issues.

voter,' a score has been calculated that compares the absolute mean distance between representatives of a particular party and their party voters with the absolute mean distance to the 'median voter.' The measure subtracts from the absolute mean distance to party voters the absolute mean distance to the 'median voter.' The distance to the 'median voter' position is calculated as the absolute mean difference between the mean position of all MPs of a particular party on an issue and the mean position of all voters on that same issue. The 'median voter' concept normally implies using the median of a distribution for comparison (Mueller 1984: 37). However, Davis, Hinich, and Ordeshook (1970: 439–43; see also Mueller 1984: 38) have shown that when equilibria exist, they are at the mean. The following restricting assumptions, however, are preconditions for applying equilibrium strategies: first, distributions are single-peaked[2] and, second, plurality maximization rather than vote maximization steers the electoral competition. This is because if winning is the criterion, a candidate must consider the votes his opponents receives as well as the votes that he receives himself. Thus the absolute difference between differences[3] is referred to as *relative distance measure*.

The second relative measure is, in Achen's terms, a responsiveness measure (Achen 1978: 490–4). It is based on an unstandardized regression coefficient (*B*) and measures the responsiveness of representatives of a party to their party voters as compared to the median voter position. It is based on the following simple regression equation:

Absolute distance to party voters = $a + b$ (absolute distance to the median voter position)

The unstandardized regression coefficient equal to 1 indicates that the distances to party voters are as large as to the median voter position. A lower coefficient indicates that the representatives represent their party voters better than the median voters. In order to have a score that is high if relative responsiveness is high, the unstandardized regression coefficient has been subtracted from 1. This is the *relative* responsiveness measure.

---

[2] Not all empirical distributions of issue positions of voters in the studies considered here are unimodal: in Germany, Sweden, and the USA 61 to 67 per cent of all issue distributions, in France and the Netherlands less than 50 per cent. However, polarized distributions (U-curved) are rare, too: none of the distributions in Germany, Sweden, and the USA, 6 per cent in the Netherlands, 20 per cent in France (see the chapter by Holmberg in this volume). Thus, the assumption of unimodality is violated for some distributions, but not in a way that would make it incongruous to stick to it.

[3] The formula simply is: absolute mean difference between representatives of a particular party to party voters minus mean difference between representatives of a particular party to the mean of the electorate.

TABLE 7.1. Number of cases for comparison of issue positions

	No. of parties	No. of issues	No. of cases for comparison		
			Electorate all MPs	Electorate/ party MPs[a]	Party voters/ party MPs
France 1968[b]	5	12	12	60	60
Germany 1988/9	4	11	11	44	44
Netherlands 1971	12	7	7	84	84
Netherlands 1977	9	5	5	45	45
Netherlands 1989	9	4	4	36	36
Sweden 1968	5	19	19	95	95
Sweden 1985	5	20	20	100	100
Sweden 1988	6	13	13	78	78
USA 1958	2	7	7	14	14
USA 1986/87		7	7	14	14
Total			105	570	570

[a] In this comparison, the MPs' position varies in every case, whereas the electorate's position varies only according to the issues.
[b] Candidate survey.

Thus, three measures for policy representation will be used: the *relative distance* and the *relative responsiveness* which aim to measure the representation of party voters as compared to the median voter, and the *absolute distance* which measures the representation of voters in absolute terms.

The standard comparison used here is that of policy distances between MPs of a particular party and that party's voters in relation to the distances between a particular party's MPs and the median voter. Consequently the units of analysis are pairs (*a*) of MPs of a particular party with party voters and (*b*) of MPs of a particular party with the *electorate*. Given the number of parties and the number of issues, the data matrix contains 570 cases of comparison between MPs and party voters and the same number of comparisons between MPs of a particular party and the electorate (see Table 7.1).

Sweden shows the maximum number of comparisons within one country, with 100 in 1985; the United States shows the minimum number in 1958 and 1986–7, with 14 possible comparisons. Most of the analysis of the impact of system characteristics will be done on the aggregate level. That is, the mean results concerning policy representation will be used as dependent variables in the case of system comparisons at the country level. Thus the analysis will contain 10 cases based on quite reliable multiple comparisons at the country level.

SYSTEM CHARACTERISTICS AND POLICY REPRESENTATION

Why should system characteristics affect political representation; and if they do, which are important? At least one can assume that there is a relationship between political performance, which includes political representation, and system characteristics, given the vast amount of literature in this field. For example, typologies of democratic systems have been used to look at the impact of systemic differences on stability and democratic quality (Lijphart 1984, 1994), where democratic quality represents formal structures (Dahl 1971: 231–45). Different system types have been evaluated with respect to the capacity of governments to maintain public order and voter participation (Powell 1986). System typologies have also been used to evaluate government performance in different terms, such as women's representation and policies, and the consequences of government politics involving economic inequality, economic growth, and so on (Lijphart 1991). There is also a large body of literature on government structures and socio-economic performance (Alvarez et al. 1991; Cusack 1997; Schmidt 1996).

Given the topic 'representation,' we must identify characteristics of a political system that affect the relationship between MPs and those they represent. Obviously, the electoral process is one of the main linkages between MPs and their constituents. Two general questions are relevant in this respect: first, what accounts for MPs' orientations toward voters; and second, what influences voters' orientations toward parties? One important determinant of an MP's orientation is how he or she has to perform in order to become re-elected. Thus the question is whether there are systemic mechanisms that demand a specific focus of representation by the MP in order to enhance the likelihood of re-election. Central questions with regard to voters in an election concern what choices exist and which choice voters eventually make. Thus, it is generally accepted that 'demand' and 'supply' factors affect policy representation. Respective 'demand' and 'supply' hypotheses will be developed in more detail as well as tested in the following sections.

THE ELECTORAL SYSTEM AND THE PARTY VS. MEDIAN VOTER EFFECT ON POLICY REPRESENTATION

A lucky circumstance for this analysis is that each of the five political systems under investigation represents a certain type of electoral system. This situation leads us to a 'quasi-experimental' design with which to estimate the impact of electoral systems on policy representation. The five systems fit nicely on a majoritarian–proportional continuum. Starting from the majoritarian pole, France is first. It has an absolute majority rule in single-member districts. On the first ballot a majority of votes is required for election; if no candidate wins a majority, a plurality suffices in the second ballot. This situation is the so-called 'Romanic majority rule' (Nohlen 1978: 155). Lijphart calls such systems mixed majority-plurality systems (Lijphart 1984: 152). The United States has a relative majority rule in single member districts, i.e. the plurality of votes is required for election (Nohlen 1978: 110 ff.). The German electoral system is in between the majoritarian and proportional systems, referred to as personalized proportional vote (Nohlen 1978: 299 ff.). In Germany voters cast two ballots simultaneously, one for a candidate to be chosen by the plurality rule in single member districts, and the other for a party list to be awarded seats by proportional representation in a state-wide multi-member district. 'Each party then gets its plurality-won seats plus the number of seats won by the proportional rule less the number of plurality-won seats' (Riker 1986: 37). Sweden and the Netherlands have a list-proportional representation but differ with respect to proportional corrections. In Sweden a special formula allows small parties to gain additional mandates from a larger party in order to make representation fairer (Nohlen 1978: 255 ff.). The most proportional system can be found in the Netherlands, with a purely proportional rule. The voter has one vote, which he casts for the leader of the list of his preferred party. Yet there is also the possibility of preference-voting for a candidate different from the first one on the list. However, de facto this preference voting has hardly any effect, since the first-placed candidates gain on average about 90 per cent of the vote.

This nice continuum from majority to proportional rule can also be regarded as a continuum from a system with personalized to a system with particized politics. The electoral law in majoritarian systems promotes the candidates: in proportional systems, the parties. For (re-)election in majoritarian systems, candidates depend mainly on the electorate. This is not to suggest that party support does not matter: however, the general difference between majoritarian and proportional systems is that a candidate represents a party, rather than several candidates from a party list. In proportional systems it is imperative that the candidate gains a favourable position on the party list. More generally, according to the 'majority control vision' of democracy, the presence of 'a party or candidate located at or very near the median voter' implies that 'strategic incentives for the parties and the rational choices of the voters act together to provide victories for the party that is closest to the median' (Huber and Powell 1994: 297). In contrast to this centre-driven electoral competition, the 'Proportionate Influence Vision' suggests that 'the parties do not—must not—converge to the centre unless virtually all the voters are located very close to it' (Huber and Powell 1994: 299). This view is also emphasized in the literature on the structure of party systems and the character of party competition. While majority rule spurs the struggle for winning the majority of one assumed normal distribution of preferences in the electorate, multiple preference distributions of the party voters can be found in proportional systems (Downs 1957: 117–27; Sartori 1976: ch. 10).

From these considerations a simple hypothesis·can be deduced: *Candidates in majority systems are more concerned with the majority of the electorate, whereas candidates on party lists are more concerned with the median party voter*. In other words: in majoritarian systems candidates focus on the 'median voter', in proportional systems, on the party voter.

However, from the point of view of a candidate in a system with majority or plurality rule, the median voter is not defined in terms of the electorate at large but in terms of much smaller electoral districts.[4] Thus, a candidate need not be concerned with the mean position of the electorate of the whole nation but of only a particular regionally defined portion of the total electorate. Hence in a political system there exist as many median voter positions as there are electoral districts. These positions can vary considerably between regions as can the degree of policy representation between electoral districts. From this observation one might conclude that the measure for the distance between MPs and voters fails to take this into account because it is based on national means. In mathematical terms the mean distance on the national level is the same as the national average of the distances calculated for all electoral districts under the following conditions: (1) the regional electoral units are one-tier districts, i.e. they are mutually exclusive (Rae 1975: 20), (2) electoral units are the same size as the number of voters, and (3) they have equal weight, i.e. the number of seats per district is equal. None of the systems under observation does not have one-tier districts with respect to the regional division of the country (Lijphart 1994: 30–9).[5] In all countries considered in this analysis, the general democratic rule is 'one man — one vote', which means in legal terms that districts have to be of the same size and weight, which is roughly the case empirically.[6] Since the conditions

---

[4] Rae (1975: 19) gives a simple and clear definition of electoral districts: 'Electoral districts are the units within which voting returns are translated into distributions of parliamentary seats. . . . Electoral districts should not be confused with voting districts . . . in which no allocation of seats takes place but in which voting returns are collected.'

[5] However, Sweden and Germany are in fact systems with two-tier districting, since the final allocation of seats takes place at a higher than the local level. But the initial allocation of seats on the local level takes place in mutually exclusive districts (Lijphart 1994: 32).

[6] However, reapportionment is a permanent problem of all democracies and used to be a severe problem, for example, in the USA in the early 1960s (Baker 1986).

TABLE 7.2. Majoritarian and proportional systems: hypothetical framework

	Majoritarian system	Proportional system
The electoral law promotes . . .	candidates	parties
The individual candidates' (re-) election mainly depends on the . . .	electorate in the district	party
Candidates are primarily oriented toward the . . .	median voter of the district	party voter
Consequence for policy representation	Distance to median voter relatively low compared with distance to party voter	Distance to party voter relatively low compared with distance to median voter

are met, it does not matter whether the distances between the elected and the electors are calculated on a district basis, added up and averaged, or whether the national means of MPs and the total electorate are compared, since both formulas are equivalent.[7] Thus, the median voter position on an issue can be measured by the national mean of the electorate.

The consequence for policy representation implied by our hypothesis is that representatives in majoritarian systems in contrast to those in proportional systems must exert more effort to minimize the distance to the median voter. Electoral rules have an impact on the focus of representation that a representative chooses: the term 'focus' here is not used exactly as it was introduced by Eulau, Wahlke, and colleagues (Eulau, Wahlke, et al. 1978), as it refers not to geographical but to electoral units. Table 7.2 gives a summary of the argument about how electoral systems affect representational focus. Again, this is not to imply that party voters do not matter to representatives in majoritarian systems or that the median voter is unimportant to representatives in proportional systems. Rather, the hypothesis points to the relative emphasis placed on both aspects of political competition. Since the five political systems under study are so properly lined up on a majoritarian-proportional continuum, one would expect that representatives in France are at one end and those in the Netherlands at the other end with regard to policy representation of the median voter's and the party voter's positions.

---

[7] The formulas are equivalent as is easily to be seen:
$$((MP_1 - E_1) + (MP_2 - E_2) + \ldots + (MP_n - E_n))/n = (MP_1 + MP_2 + \ldots + MP_n)/n - (E_1 + E_2 + \ldots + E_n)/n$$
where MP is the mean position of MPs; E the mean position of voters, the subscript indicates the district, n is the number of districts.

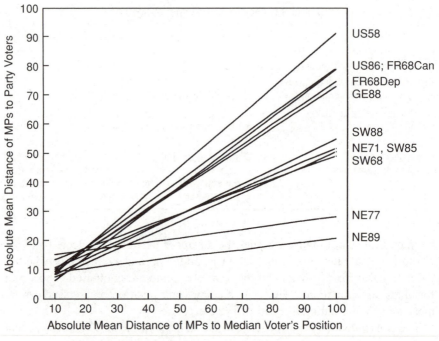

F IG . 7.1. Party vs. median voter effect on policy representation

In order to measure the *relative distance*, that is, whether MPs are closer to the median voter or to their party voters, the two absolute distance measures have been put into relationship. To compare the *relative responsiveness* towards party voters and towards median voters, we take up Achen's proposal (Achen 1978: 490) and use the regression approach. Scatterplotting the two distances, that is, the policy distance of the MPs of a particular party to both the median voter's position and to that of their party voters, the regression line should be close to the diagonal in majoritarian systems, whereas in proportional systems the regression line should be closer to the axis of distance to the median voter's position, indicating that the within-party distance is comparatively smaller. If the distance of MPs' positions to the median voter's position is represented on the X-axis and the distance to the party voters on the Y-axis, one would, in terms of a regression analysis, expect that the magnitude of change in Y is larger in the highly majoritarian system and smaller in the strongly proportional system. The result is shown in Figure 7.1.

The B-coefficient thus is kind of a trade-off measure. This differs from Achen's proposed responsiveness measure (Achen 1978), since it does not set up a relationship between representatives and represented, but instead measures distances of representatives to two different electoral units. The B-coefficient measures the relative advantage of party voters over the median voter with respect to policy representation. We call it therefore *relative* responsiveness.

The rank order of countries with respect to the magnitude of change in Y (the distance to party voters) matches the electoral system-order described above almost perfectly: the two majoritarian systems rank highest, followed by Germany with its mixed system of one vote for a candidate and one vote for a party list, then Sweden; the Netherlands rank lowest as it is the most proportional system, with the exception of 1971, where it was close to Sweden. Thus the hypothesis is confirmed in general terms.

None the less, the rank order does not completely correspond to that in our hypothesis—(France, the USA, Germany, Sweden, the Netherlands), because the United States ranks above France. Given that the hypothesis is based on a rough estimation of the electoral systems, we must look more systematically at the structure of the political systems, based on macro-data indicators. Lijphart has come up with several indicators classifying democratic political systems on the majoritarian–consensual dimension. A fundamental work on this topic is the book *Democracies*, in which Lijphart develops the empirical indicators that he further refines in later works (Lijphart 1984: 211 ff.). His empirical indicators provide more systematic information about the mechanisms and the dominance of majoritarian structures compared with proportional structures in the political system. Looking at Lijphart's indicators, we first observe that the preliminary rank order of countries on the majoritarian–proportional dimension needs modification. Lijphart's consensus scores, developed on the basis of the indicators found in *Democracies* (1984: 216) and refined in Lijphart and Crepaz (1991), classify the United States as least consensual or most majoritarian, followed by France, Germany, Sweden, and the Netherlands. Thus, the rank order of countries with respect to the relative advantage of the median voter over the party voter is exactly the same as the rank order proposed by Lijphart and Crepaz.

The correlation of the consensus score and relative responsiveness of Lijphart and Crepaz most obviously shows the effect of system character-istics on policy representation. The correlation coefficient of the aggregated data for the ten representation studies is as high as 0.91 and statistically highly significant. The scatterplot of both variables shows a clear pattern. Where proportionality is lowest, relative responsiveness to party voters is also low-est, as reflected by the location of the United States for the years 1958 and 1986. Relative responsiveness is highest where proportionality is highest, as evidenced by the Netherlands in 1977 and 1989. In 1971 the Netherlands is

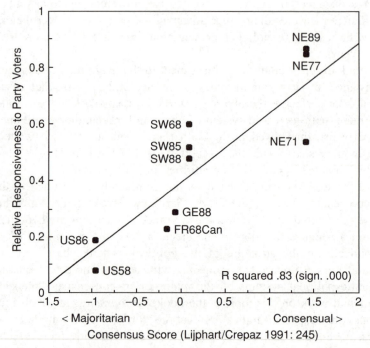

FIG. 7.2. Consensus and relative responsiveness to party voters

somewhat of an outlier. The reason may be due to the disturbances and turbulences within the political and party systems at that time. The peak of the deconfessionalization process lay between 1967 and 1972 (Middendrop 1991: 16): the electoral turnout in 1971 was about 15 percentage points lower than in any election since the Second World War and, except for 1994, the lowest in any Dutch elections. France, Germany, and Sweden rank in between according to their degree of proportionality (Figure 7.2). Explained variance of relative responsiveness to party voters is 83 per cent.

The correlation of relative distance to party voters and the consensus score is also high, but negative (−0.70). The negative correlation with the relative distance measure and the positive correlation with the relative responsiveness measure clearly indicate that the more proportional, or in Lijphart's terms, 'consensual', a political system, the better represented are party voters' positions as compared with the median voter's position. The results so far have been based solely on the one indicator of Lijphart and Crepaz (1991). In order to check the validity of the results, other measures characterizing the electoral system have been introduced. Disproportionality of election results is most closely related to the majoritarian-proportional dimension. We have

TABLE 7.3. System characteristics and the party vs. median voter policy representation

	Comparative advantage of party voters over the median voter position	
	Relative distance	Relative responsiveness
Consensus score[a]	−0.70 (0.012)	0.91 (0.000)
Average disproportionality[b]	0.66 (0.018)	−0.83 (0.001)
Disproportionality (electorate)[c]	0.58 (0.040)	−0.75 (0.007)
Disproportionality (valid votes)[d]	0.53 (0.056)	−0.44 (0.104)

Aggregate correlations, 10 cases; in brackets: significance (p).

Sources/Measures:
[a] Lijphart and Crepaz 1991: 245.
[b] Average 1945–90; Volkens 1995: 41*a*.
[c] Relations seat to votes; calculations are based on the electorate as a whole. Macro Databank Political Systems, WZB, Institutions and Social Change.
[d] Relations seat to votes; calculations are based on valid votes. Macro Databank Political Systems, WZB, Institutions and Social Change.

checked for three different measures of proportionality: the average disproportionality of the electoral law of a country between 1945 and 1990 and the disproportionality of an electoral law at the election preceding the respective representation study in a country, based on the electorate as well as on valid votes only.

The correlation coefficients for the relationship between disproportionality measures and relative distance show a positive sign, of course, since the higher the disproportionality, the stronger the orientation towards the median voter. The correlations with relative responsiveness are negative, as expected. All correlations strongly support the results already found with respect to the consensus score (Table 7.3). Thus in substantive terms, the hypothesis is supported: the more majoritarian a system, the more MPs represent the median voter position and vice versa; the more proportional a system, the more closely are MPs matched with their party voters.

PARTY SYSTEM AND POLICY REPRESENTATION: THE SUPPLY EXPLANATION

Having looked at the mechanisms influencing MPs' focus of representation and thereby policy representation, we turn now to what choices a party system offers to the voter, and how the voter's choice may influence policy representation. Bearing this in mind, Eckstein states that the 'subject of party

systems is concerned with the interaction patterns among significant electoral organizations . . . defining *choices* that can be resolved by the electoral
process' (Eckstein 1968: 438). One can conceptualize the electoral mechanism as a model of spatial competition between parties in which the voters'
perceptions of each party's position determine their choice (for a similar
conceptualization but at the candidate level see Davis et al. 1970: 426).

Since voters have divergent interests (Downs 1957: 154 ff.), the party
system should meet this divergence at least in normative terms of representation theory by offering an adequate amount of choices. This assumption
refers both to the kind and to the number of interests represented by the party
system. If there is a sufficient variety of choices in the party system, the voter
can make a perfect choice—he can find a party close to him or her in terms
of policy positions. However, a complete match is unlikely. Thus the voter
will vote for the party nearest to him or her (Robertson 1976: 27). Assuming
this more realistic case of optimal choice rather than perfect choice, the degree
to which voters and parties match could strongly depend on the scope of choices
offered. If there are too few choices compared to the diverse interests of
the electorate, then the match is bound to be less adequate than in a party
system where political choices are more differentiated.

Thus a simple argument relates the scope of choices offered by the party
system to policy representation: the more differentiated the supply, that is,
the choices offered, the more likely it is that a voter will find a supply that
best fits her or his own interest. The more divergent the policy packages
are (Davis et al. 1970: 426), the more specific, that is, the better a voter's
choice can be. The hypothesis on policy representation is straightforward: *the
more divergent the political supply, the better the choice of the voters and
therefore the closer the policy positions of voters of a particular party and
the MPs of that particular party.*

The supply of a party system can be measured in different ways. The range
of generalized political positions of parties in a party system is a measure
that is generally referred to as polarization. Polarization in a party system
provides a general tool for measuring the relationship of political parties
to one another in political terms (Sartori 1976: 44). This is the perspective
of competition and thus the perspective of the parties or party politicians.
From the voter's point of view, polarization indicates supply and possible
choices that can be made. In most cases polarization measures refer to the
distribution of parties on a left–right dimension. There are simple as well as
complex measures of polarization. The most simple though efficient measure
is to look at the range of a party system—that is, the range between the
two most extreme positions on the left and on the right. This is often done
on the basis of the perceptions of voters. In order to have an independent

measurement of the party system rather than a measure based on the perception of the voters, the left–right ranges calculated here utilize expert left–right party placements provided by a study conducted by Huber and Inglehart (1995).

Other more complex measures place parties' locations in a political space in relation to one another. Although misleading, these measures are also referred to as polarization. What they really indicate, in contrast to the left–right range score of a party system, is the degree of differentiation of political supply within the party system, rather than pure polarization. Most often they are calculated on the basis of left–right scores of parties. Since we deal here with policy representation with respect to specific issues rather than with left–right orientations, we make use of a measurement based on the content of party election platforms. Although parties' positions on issues in the party platforms have been re-specified in terms of left and right, the measurement is more comprehensive than a pretend left–right scale. This measurement re-specifies a multidimensional issue space on a single generalized dimension. The scores have been combined into a measure of political differentiation that takes into account the different weights of parties, as determined by their electoral and parliamentary strength (Macro Databank Political Systems, WZB, Institutions and Social Change).

The hypothesis put forward here suggests that the higher the differentiation of the political supply, the closer is the match between MPs of a particular party and that party's voters, both in relative terms—compared with the policy representation of the median voter's position—and in absolute terms. With regard first to polarization of the party system and its impact on the party voter versus median voter effect, empirical results strongly support the hypothesis. The scatterplot of programmatic polarization of party systems in terms of their left–right ranges and relative responsiveness to party voters shows a strong relationship. The stronger the polarization—the more differentiated the supply—the better the match between party voters and MPs of that party, as compared with median voter policy representation. The two studies from the United States rank lowest, both with respect to polarization and relative responsiveness to party voters, while the Dutch studies of 1977 and 1989 rank highest in both respects. As seen before, 1971 is a special point in time in the development of the Dutch political system and thus lies somewhat apart from the regression line. Germany, France, and Sweden rank between the United States and the Netherlands, with medium polarization and medium relative responsiveness. The explained variance of the regression analysis is 76 per cent and statistically significant (see Figure 7.3). The correlation between polarization and the relative distance to party voters is negative and also quite high (−0.64, see Table 7.4).

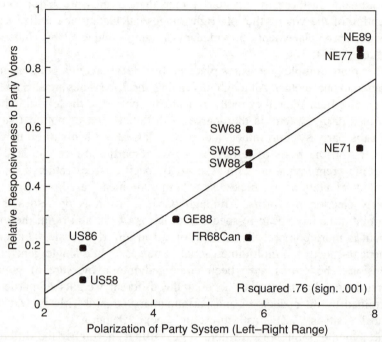

FIG. 7.3. Party system polarization and party vs. median voter effect

TABLE 7.4. Political supply and policy representation of party voters as compared to the median voter

	Comparative advantage of party voters over the median voter	
	Relative distance	Relative responsiveness
Programmatic differentiation of the party system[a]	−0.53 (0.057)	0.59 (0.036)
Programmatic differentiation of the parliamentary parties[a]	−0.63 (0.026)	0.67 (0.016)
Polarization of the parliamentary parties (L–R-Range)[b]	−0.64 (0.024)	0.87 (0.001)
Number of parliamentary parties	−0.55 (0.051)	0.75 (0.006)

Aggregate correlations, 10 cases; in brackets: significance (*p*).

Sources/Measures:
[a] Based on programmatic left—right positions of party election manifestoes. Macro Databank Political Systems, WZB Institutions and Social Change.
[b] Range of parliamentary parties on a 10-point left–right scale; expert rating of parties. Huber and Inglehart 1995.

The results regarding the relationship between programmatic differentiation of the party system and relative responsiveness as well as relative distance point toward the same direction. Correlations are somewhat lower but still high, with the smallest still higher than 0.5. The programmatic differentiation of the party system as a whole seems to be a little less related to relative responsiveness than the programmatic differentiation of the parties in parliament. For both of them, correlations with relative responsiveness are positive, with relative distance negative, but in absolute terms they are about 0.10 higher for programmatic differentiation of parties in parliament. This result indicates that in particular the programmatic differentiation of those parties that also have a chance to enter parliament is related to the quality of policy representation of party voters. It is also obvious from Table 7.4 that this is not an effect of the number of parties, rather, it depends very much on whether parties really do offer different political positions. Since the correlations of numbers of parties in parliament and the relative measures of policy representation are high, one can easily assume that there is in reality a high correspondence of numbers of parties, i.e. fragmentization, and polarization or differentiation of political supply. But correlations are not in every case as high as for the measures of political supply, showing that there is no identity of differentiation of supply and numbers of parties (Table 7.4).

Turning to the relationship between the differentiation of political supply and the absolute match between the voters and MPs of a particular party, the hypothesis suggests that policy representation is not only better in relative but also in absolute terms. That is, instead of an international comparison of measures based on within-country differences between median and party voters we now consider a comparison of absolute measures of distances between MPs and party voters across countries. Given the problem that the studies under investigation represent different issues, scalings, and points in time, an absolute comparison might be regarded as problematic. On the other hand, the standardizations used here should minimize, although not totally filter out, the effects of different designs. Thus, what can be done is only a tentative assessment of the quality of party voter's policy representation across countries. However, even if the differences between studies make the comparison on the absolute level more difficult, empirically the relationship postulated in the hypothesis should show up, although probably not unaffected by these difficulties.

Empirical results regarding the differentiation of political supply and the absolute measure for policy representation support the hypothesis. Although results are not as convincing as for the two relative measures, they clearly point toward the same direction. The scatterplot of programmatic differentiation of parliamentary parties and the mean distances between MPs of a

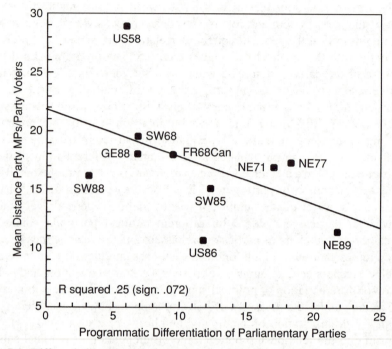

FIG. 7.4. Differentiation of programmatic supply and policy representation of party voters

particular party and their voters show a clear pattern. Countries with high programmatic differentiation show the lowest distance, countries with low programmatic differentiation show the highest distance. As could be expected from the difficulties arising from a comparison of such divergent representation studies like those used here, some of the studies are off the regression line. But explained variance still accounts for 25 per cent and statistical significance is, given the small numbers of cases, not totally poor (Figure 7.4).

Since the distance measure ranges from 0 to 100 it is easy to interpret in percentages any mismatch between MPs and their voters. The empirical range is between 10 per cent and about 30 per cent of maximum possible distance. Thus, a complete match between elected and electors is not what can be expected, a point which is very often made in the literature on political representation. However, there are clear variations in the degree of distance that can be related to the differentiation of political supply. This is also obvious from the correlation between measures of political supply other than the one in the scatterplot. The programmatic differentiation of the party system at large matters almost as much. The sheer left–right range of

TABLE 7.5. Political supply and policy representation of party voters in absolute measures

	Absolute mean difference party MPs/party voters
Programmatic differentiation of the party system	−0.49 (.074)
Programmatic differentiation of the parliamentary parties	−0.50 (.072)
Polarization of the parliamentary parties (L–R-Range)	−0.34 (.171)
Number of parliamentary parties	−0.29 (.210)

Aggregate correlations, 10 cases; in brackets: significance (*p*).
Sources/Measures: see Table 7.4.

parliamentary parties (polarization) as well as the number of parliamentary parties are not that closely related to the distances between MPs of a particular party and their voters but the range and the number of parties do not disturb the pattern either (Table 7.5).

Thus, the hypothesis that political supply affects the quality of policy representation of party voters is sustained in general terms. The choices offered to the voters seem to matter much in terms of the electoral link. In an indirect way results also support the notion that there is some rationality behind voting decision mechanisms. If voters did not vote for what can be regarded as an optimal choice in terms of policy distances, the result would then differ very much from ours. In theoretical terms, that supports the general notion that the electoral link may be the most important link between representatives and represented in terms of policy representation.

SUMMARY OF FINDINGS

This chapter is an attempt to study the effect of differences in the structure of political systems on policy representation. On the basis of ten representation studies for five polities—France, Germany, the Netherlands, Sweden, and the United States of America, each of which represents a different political system—the influence of system characteristics on policy representation has been investigated in two different dimensions: the character of the electoral systems and the supply side of the political system in terms of the programmatic differentiation of political parties. It was hypothesized that the character of electoral systems affects the focus of representation of MPs and that the differentiation of political supply affects the voter's choice.

With respect to electoral systems, each of the five polities represents a certain point on a continuum from majoritarian to proportional or consensual democratic systems. It was argued that in order to win the majority or at least the plurality of votes in majoritarian systems, candidates are more concerned with the dominant position of the electorate. In contrast, candidates in proportional systems are more concerned with party voters, since (re-)election depends much more on the party due to the list system. Empirical results on policy representation measured by distances in policy positions of MPs and voters clearly show that the median voter is relatively better off in majoritarian systems, while the party voter is better off in proportional systems. Thus, the hypothesized difference in policy representation between personalized and particized electoral systems shows up clearly.

With regard to the political supply side, we hypothesized that the more differentiated the supply, the better the possible choices for voters. The differentiation of policy offers was measured in terms of polarization and programmatic differentiation as expressed in election manifestos. Empirically, results show that the supply side of the political system has a positive effect on policy representation. In relative terms, party voters are clearly better off than median voters in systems with large differentiation of political supply. In absolute terms of the size of policy distances between MPs and voters, party voters are better off in those countries where political supply is more differentiated.

Results demonstrate clearly that the way the electoral link is constructed in legal terms as well as its character in terms of content, that is, political supply, affect policy representation strongly. Viewed from above it is the electoral system that affects policy representation. Viewed from the base, it is the opportunity for optimal choice that affects the quality of policy representation. The direction of this influence is obvious: the more proportional a system and the more differentiated the political supply offered by political parties, the better the policy representation of party voters. To take up the cudgels for proportional systems in contrast to majoritarian systems would be too strong a conclusion. Political systems are characterized by different forms of bias: proportional systems by the bias of better parliamentary policy representation, and majoritarian systems by the bias of more efficient government. Raising one system over the other is a normative question.

REFERENCES

Achen, Christopher, H. (1977), 'Measuring Representation: Perils of the Correlation Coefficient', *American Journal of Political Science*, 21: 805–15.

—— (1978), 'Measuring Representation', *American Journal of Political Science*, 22: 475–510.

Alvarez, R. Michael, Garrett, Geoffrey, and Lange, Peter (1991), 'Government Partisanship, Labor Organization, and Macroeconomic Performance', *American Political Science Review*, 85: 539–56.

Baker, Gordon E. (1986), 'Whatever Happened to the Reapportionment Revolution in the United States?', in Grofman and Lijphart 1986: 257–76.

Barnes, Samuel (1977), *Representation in Italy: Institutionalized Tradition and Electoral Choice* (Chicago: University of Chicago Press).

Converse, Philip E., and Pierce, Roy (1986), *Political Representation in France* (Cambridge, Mass.: Harvard University Press).

Cox, Gary W. (1997), *Making Votes Count* (Cambridge: Cambridge University Press).

Cusack, Thomas R. (1997), 'Partisan Politics and Public Finance', *Public Choice*, 91: 375–95.

Dahl, Robert A. (1971), *Polyarchy: Participation and Opposition* (New Haven: Yale University Press).

—— (1989), *Democracy and its Critics* (New Haven: Yale University Press).

Dalton, Russell J. (1985), 'Political Parties and Political Representation: Party Supporters and Party Elites in Nine Nations', *Comparative Political Studies*, 18: 267–99.

Davis, Otto, Hinich, Melvin J., and Ordeshook, Peter C. (1970), 'An Expository Development of a Mathematical Model of the Electoral Process', *American Political Science Review*, 26: 426–48.

Downs, Anthony (1957), *An Economic Theory of Democracy* (New York: Harper & Row).

Eckstein, Harry (1968), 'Party Systems' in David L. Sills (ed.), *International Encyclopedia of the Social Sciences*, vol. xvii (New York: MacMillan/Free Press), 436–53.

Eulau, Heinz (1978), 'Changing Views of Representation', in Eulau, Wahlke et al. 1978: 31–54.

—— (1987), 'Converse and Pierce on Representation in France: The Congruence Model Revisited', *Legislative Studies Quarterly*, 12: 171–214.

—— and Prewitt, Kenneth (1973), *Labyrinths of Democracy: Adaptations, Linkages, Representation and Policies in Urban Politics* (New York: Bobbs-Merril Co.).

—— and Wahlke, John C. (1978), 'Some Empirical Observations on the Theory of Edmund Burke', in Eulau, Wahlke, et al. 1978: 111–26.

—— Wahlke, John C., et al. (1978), *The Politics of Representation* (London: Sage).

Farah, Barbara G. (1980), 'Political Representation in West Germany: The Institution and Maintenance of Mass–Elite Linkages', Ph.D. diss., University of Michigan.

Grofman, Bernard, and Lijphart, Arend (eds.) (1986), *Electoral Laws and Their Political Consequences* (New York: Agathon Press).

Herrera, Cheryl Lyn, Herrera, Richard, and Smith, Eric R. A. N. (1992), 'Public Opinion and Congressional Representation', *Public Opinion Quarterly*, 56: 185–205.

Herzog, Dietrich, Rebenstorf, Hilke, Werner, Camilla, and Wessels, Bernhard (1990), *Abgeordnete und Bürger* (Opladen: Westdeutscher Verlag).

Holmberg, Sören (1989), 'Political Representation in Sweden', *Scandinavian Political Studies*, 12: 1–36.

Huber, John, and Inglehart, Ronald (1995), 'Expert Interpretations of Party Space and Party Locations in 42 Societies', *Party Politics*, 1: 73–112.

—— and Powell, G. Bingham (1994), 'Congruence between Citizens and Policy-makers in Two Visions of Liberal Democracy', *World Politics*, 46: 291–326.

Irwin, Galen A., and Thomassen, Jacques (1975), 'Issue-Consensus in a Multi-party System: Voters and Leaders in the Netherlands', *Acta Politica*, 10: 389–420.

Jackson, John E., and King, David C. (1989), 'Public Goods, Private Interests, and Representation', *American Political Science Review*, 83: 1143–64.

Klingemann, Hans-Dieter, Hofferbert, Richard, and Budge, Ian (1994), *Parties, Policies and Democracy* (Boulder, Colo.: Westview Press).

Lijphart, Arend (1968), *The Politics of Accommodation* (Berkeley and Los Angeles: University of California Press).

—— (1984), *Democracies: Patterns of Majoritarian and Consensus Government in Twenty-one Countries* (New Haven: Yale University Press).

—— (1991), 'Constitutional Choices for New Democracies', *Journal of Democracy*, 2: 72–84.

—— (1994), *Electoral Systems and Party Systems* (Oxford: Oxford University Press).

—— and Crepaz, Markus M. L. (1991), 'Corporatism and Consensus Democracy in Eighteen Countries: Conceptual and Empirical Linkages', *British Journal for Political Science*, 21: 235–56.

Middentrop, C. P. (1991), *Ideology in Dutch Politics* (Assen/Maastricht: Van Gorcum).

Miller, Warren E. (1988), *Without Consent: Mass-Elite Linkages in Presidential Politics* (Lexington: University Press of Kentucky).

—— and Stokes, Donald E. (1963), 'Constituency Influence in Congress', *American Political Science Review*, 57: 45–56.

Mueller, Dennis C. (1984), 'Public Choice: A Survey', in James M. Buchanan and Robert D. Tollison (eds.), *The Theory of Public Choice II* (Ann Arbor: University of Michigan Press), 23–67.

Nohlen, Dieter (1978), *Wahlsysteme der Welt* (Munich: Piper).

Pitkin, Hannah F. (1967), *The Concept of Representation* (Berkeley and Los Angeles: University of California Press).

Porter, Stephen R. (1995), 'Political Representation in Germany: The Effects of the Candidate Selection Committees', Ph.D. diss., University of Rochester, New York.

Powell, G. Bingham (1986), 'American Voter Turnout in Comparative Perspective', *American Political Science Review*, 80: 17–41.

Rae, Douglas W. (1975), *The Political Consequences of Electoral Laws* (New Haven: Yale University Press).

Riker, William H. (1986), 'Duverger's Law Revisited', in Grofman and Lijphart 1986: 19–42.

Robertson, David (1976), *A Theory of Party Competition* (London/New York: John Wiley & Sons).

Sartori, Giovanni (1976), *Parties and Party Systems* (Cambridge: Cambridge University Press).

Schmidt, Manfred G. (1996), 'When Parties Matter', *European Journal of Political Research*, 30: 155–83.

Stinchcombe, Arthur L. (1975), 'Social Structure and Politics', in Fred I. Greenstein and Nelon W. Polsby (eds.), *Macropolitical Theory, Handbook of Political Science*, iii (Reading, Mass.: Addison-Wesley), 557–622.

Sullivan, J. L., and O'Connor, R. E. (1972), 'Electoral Choice and Popular Control of Public Policy', *American Political Science Review*, 66: 1256–68.

Taylor, Peter J., Gudgin, Graham, and Johnson, R. J. (1986), 'The Geography of Representation: "A Review of Recent Findings"', in Grofman and Lijphart 1986: 183–92.

Volkens, Andrea (1995), 'Sozio-ökonomische Polarisierung zwischen Parteien, Regierung und Opposition und Regierungswechsel in den OECD-Staaten 1945 bis 1990', Inaugural Ph.D. diss., Berlin University.

Weissberg, Robert (1978), 'Collective Versus Dyadic Representation in Congress', *American Political Science Review*, 72: 535–47.

Wessels, Bernhard (1991), 'Abgeordnete und Bürger: Parteien und Wahlkreiskommunikation als Faktoren politischer Repräsentation', in Hans-Dieter Klingemann, Richard Stöss, and Bernhard Wessels (eds.), *Politische Klasse und politische Institutionen* (Opladen: Westdeutscher Verlag), 325–56.

—— (1993), 'Politische Repräsentation: Kommunikation als Transmissionsriemen alter und neuer Politik', in Dietrich Herzog, Hilke Rebenstorf, and Bernhard Wessels (eds.), *Parlament und Gesellschaft* (Opladen: Westdeutscher Verlag).

Conclusion
Mixed Signals

Roy Pierce

This book originated in a situation that was simultaneously a remarkable opportunity and a powerful constraint. The situation was the availability of matching elite and mass data sets from five countries recording elite opinion and popular opinion on current political issues in each country. More often than not, in each country, mass and elite opinions on a given issue were expressed in identical form.

The opportunity, of course, lay in the potential for comparing the countries involved (and their respective component institutional arrangements) with regard to the degree of congruence between mass and elite opinion on the same issues. To that extent, there was the possibility for carrying out comparative studies of political representation.

The element of constraint lay in the fact that the data available for comparison related almost exclusively to elite and mass opinion on issues of current importance in each country. We had only incomplete matching data relating to mass perceptions of elite opinion or elite perceptions of mass opinion, and while we did have the indispensable data about mass partisan electoral choices, we did not have relevant data relating to elite political behaviour. In terms of the paradigmatic Miller–Stokes design for the study of representation, to which Pierce refers early in his contribution, we were required to concentrate our attention on the relationship between elite opinion and mass opinion on identical issues (what Converse and Pierce 1986: ch. 16, refer to as the AB bond).

This constraint proved to be a powerful factor in giving unity and coherence to this book. In one form or another, and by one means or another, we try to chart (and understand) the degree of congruence there is between elite and mass opinion on identical political issues, across a cluster of countries displaying diverse institutional structures, party systems, and electoral systems.

We make no pretence of trying to compare the entire, composite representation process derivable from the Miller–Stokes design across five political systems. We do believe, however, that we have furthered the analysis of one critical component of political representation—mass–elite issue linkages—in several important ways.

One important feature of our collective accomplishment is the extent to which we demonstrate the multiple ways in which mass–elite opinion congruence may be conceptualized and measured.

Most of the contributions at some point compare mean mass issue positions with mean elite positions, by political party (based on party affiliation for the elites and partisan vote for the mass), but that method is not followed uniformly. Wessels gives considerable attention to median positions as well as to mean positions, both by party affiliation and overall. Holmberg directly compares the shapes of the actual raw distributions (based on proportions), at the mass and elite levels, of the scale scores employed in the matching surveys from which the data were obtained. Pierce also employs proportions in his analysis, by computing what proportion of the voters for each party held a position on each issue that was closer to the mean position on the same issue of the party for which they voted than it was to the mean position on the issue of any other party. Congruence turns out, on reflection, to be a complex, many-faceted notion.

In whatever form in which it has been expressed in this book, congruence also appears not to be strikingly high. Of course, congruence is a relative term, but the contributions that deal directly with this issue are not impressed with the levels of mass–elite issue congruence they encountered. Esaiasson, who focuses on regional variations in mass opinion, finds little in the way of matching variations on the elite side. Pierce quantifies the limits of the range within which the levels of congruence (as he measures it) can fall and finds that those observed seldom rise above what chance alone would produce. At the same time, however, he finds that of all the issues covered, ideology—expressed as self-locations on the left–right scale for the European countries and on the liberal–conservative scale for the United States—enjoys higher levels of congruence than do the specific policy measures. Holmberg goes so far as to hold that random selection of deputies would produce closer issue congruence (as he measures it) within our sample of political systems than the various electoral processes actually employed across our universe of countries have done thus far.

These contributions reflect due concern for the importance of standardization of relevant measures when doing cross-national analysis. Holmberg offers some judicious considerations in this regard along with his conduct of certain key analyses both with and without standardization of particular measures.

Wessels pays close attention to standardization of measures *across* the entire panoply of national data sets. Pierce standardizes the base data *within* national sets, in order to emphasize relative congruence over absolute congruence, and he also controls for the size of the party system in estimating levels of congruence by country.

Given our findings of comparatively low levels of mass–elite issue congruence, however measured, the contributions of Thomassen and Herrera are particularly apt. They both consider the central issue of the extent to which political communication promotes or impedes such issue congruence. Specifically, Herrera investigates whether the left–right dimension is interpreted in the same way by masses and elites in the United States and the Netherlands. Thomassen examines on a broader comparative basis the extent to which left–right self-locations are correlated with more specific issue positions among masses and elites. Herrera is more sanguine than Thomassen with regard to the usefulness of the left–right dimension in promoting congruence, but both chapters provide ample reason for avoiding excessive expectations about it.

The diverse institutional characteristics of our universe of political systems almost automatically leads to the question of whether those specific arrangements—whether the constitutional system, the party system, or the electoral system—have discernible effects on the levels and character of mass–elite issue congruence. Here the line is sharpest between Wessels, who argues that institutions do count, and Holmberg, who insists that they do not. To complicate the situation further, Pierce implies that institutions count but suggests that the outcomes are the reverse of those indicated by Wessels. We leave it to our readers to arbitrate among these alternatives.

To the extent that this volume revolves around a central theoretical theme, therefore, it has been a critical examination of the responsible party model of issue representation. That familiar model is more closely associated with some of the political systems we have examined than with others. Sweden and the Netherlands fit the terms of the model most closely; the United States fits it least closely. It is, therefore, reasonable for us to ask the following question. Is the responsible party model consistent with our empirical findings concerning the levels of mass–elite issue congruence?

Holmberg and Pierce answer with a resounding 'No!'. Thomassen does not address the issue quite as directly as they do, but he is surely sceptical about its applicability in the current conditions of mass–elite communication. Wessels does not pronounce on the issue directly, but his analysis contains more support for the model than the others cited in this paragraph could find. Once again, we refer such evidence of our respective findings as we have been able to muster to our sagacious readers, who will—as is proper—have the last word.

In closing, we want to emphasize that we do not pretend to have exhausted the potential usefulness of the data that were employed in the preparation of this book. As we noted in the opening pages, the book evolved as our personal research interests intersected, converged, or diverged throughout a loosely connected series of meetings that spanned almost a decade. Other scholars, bringing different perspectives to bear on the same data, might well uncover ways in which characteristic political institutions shape mass–elite issue congruence that we have overlooked. We hope that this book will encourage at least some of our readers to utilize the extraordinarily rich data bases that are available for secondary analysis and pursue further our efforts in the cross-national study of political representation.

Appendix

Data for the Dutch Representation Studies can be found on page 54. Data for the 1992 US mass sample can be found on page 83.

DATA FROM THE UNITED STATES

The data used by the authors of this volume came, in part, from nine studies conducted in the United States. Four of the surveys are of the elite in America, defined as candidates for or members of the House of Representatives as well as delegates to the national political party nominating conventions. The surveys of the mass public are all from the American National Election Studies series. This appendix is designed to provide information about the surveys from which the data are derived and indicate where scholars may obtain the data.

The first set of data is from the 1958 American Representation Study conducted by Warren Miller and Donald Stokes. All of the respondents were either candidates for or members of the House of Representatives during the 1958 congressional elections. A total of 285 candidates from 151 congressional districts were sampled with 251 individuals taking part in the survey. The mass-level survey used in conjunction with the American Representation Study includes 1,450 respondents to the 1958 American Election Study. In both surveys, measures were derived to estimate the positions of respondents on issues such as social welfare, foreign involvement, and civil rights.

Three additional sets of American mass survey data come from the 1986, 1988, and 1992 American National Election Studies (ANES). These studies are national surveys carried out by the Survey Research Center or by the Center for Political Studies of the Institute for Social Research at the University of Michigan and date back to 1952. The surveys are based on multistage representative cross-section samples of citizens of voting age, living in private households. Each study contains information from personal interviews conducted with 1,000 to 2,000 respondents about social backgrounds, enduring political predispositions, social and political values, perceptions and evaluations of groups and candidates, opinions on questions of public policy, and participation in political life. In the 1986 ANES, there were 2,167 respondents; in 1988 there were a total of 2,040 respondents; and, in 1992, 2,485 citizens were interviewed. The fourth mass-level survey used is the American National Election Study/Senate Election Study conducted in 1988. This data collection, focusing on Senate elections, is a part of a three-part series (1988, 1990, 1992) of Senate studies. Over the course of these three elections voters in each of the 50 states were interviewed, and data were gathered on citizen evaluations of all senators at three stages of their six-year election cycles. Both survey data and contextual data for all 50 states are included. There were 3,145 respondents.

In addition to the 1958 American Representation Study, three other surveys of political elites were used in the analyses presented in this book. One of those surveys was of members of the United States House of Representatives conducted by Eric R. A. N. Smith, Richard Herrera, and Cheryl Herrera. That self-administered mail questionnaire was conducted in May and June of 1987 and includes 126 respondents, for a response rate of 29 percent. Representatives were asked a series of questions about political issues and ideology designed to match items contained in the 1986 ANES. Information about this data can be obtained by contacting Richard Herrera.

The two other sets of elite-level data come from the 1988 and 1992 Convention Delegate Studies. These data represent the fourth and fifth in a series of data collection efforts begun in 1972 to gather information on the careers and political perspectives of the delegates to the Democratic and Republican National Conventions. Respondents were also asked questions regarding their political participation and preferences, life histories, political goals and expectations, and affiliations with various groups in society. The data for the 1988 Convention Delegate Study, conducted by Warren Miller and M. Kent Jennings, were collected via self-administered questionnaires mailed to all delegates who attended the 1988 Democratic and Republican national conventions, as well as those delegates who were respondents to previous surveys of delegates. The survey took place in the first three months of 1989 and there were a total of 4,809 respondents. The 1992 Convention delegate Study was conducted by Richard Herrera and Warren Miller in Spring 1993 and Winter 1994 and included a total of 2,853 delegates who responded to the mail survey.

The following data may be obtained through the InterUniversity Consortium for Political and Social Research at the University of Michigan using the study identification numbers listed:

Survey	ICPSR Study Number
1958 American Representation Study	7226, 7292, 7293
1958 American Election Study	7215
1986 American National Election Study	8678
1988 American National Election Study	9196
1988 American National Election Study, Senate	9580
1992 American National Election Study	6067
1988 Convention Delegate Study	6366
1992 Convention Delegate Study	6353

THE FRENCH DATA

The French data used in this book derive from the data sets relating to the 1967 French legislative elections that were originally used by Philip E. Converse and Roy Pierce for their book *Political Representation in France* (1986). Post-electoral interviews were conducted with some 2000 registered voters, selected within a sample framework of 86 electoral districts, and matching interviews were conducted with 272 of the principal candidates who had competed at the same election for seats from the same 86 sample districts. The appendices of *Political Representation in France* (1986) contain detailed accounts of the design and implementation of the mass interviewing, the structure of the elite sample, and the questionnaires that were employed.

The 1967 mass data have been archived under the title *French National Election Study, 1967* (ICPSR 7372) and are available for secondary analysis through the Inter-University Consortium for Political and Social Research at the University of Michigan.

The 1967 elite data have not been archived. Efforts are under way to make these data available for further scholarly research under the stringent conditions that are essential to maintain the confidentiality of the responses.

SWEDISH REPRESENTATION STUDIES

The Swedish data used in this book originate from a series of representation studies performed in the years 1968/69, 1985, 1988, and 1994 under the auspices of the Swedish Election Studies Program. In all cases, the data consist of a study including members of the Riksdag and interviews with a sample of eligible voters. The first Riksdag Study in 1969, directed by Bo Särlvik, Per-Anders Roth and Sören Holmberg, and including Aage Clausen and Warren Miller as American collaborators, involved personal interviews with all members of the Second Chamber in the then bicameral Riksdag. The response rate was a satisfying 97 percent. The studies in 1985, 1988, and 1994 were directed by Peter Esaiasson and Sören Holmberg and were done by mail questionnaires sent to all members of the now unicameral Riksdag. The response rate were still 97 percent in all three surveys.

The election surveys in the years 1968, 1985, 1988, and 1994 all comprised samples of about 3,600 eligible voters, 18–80 years old. Face-to-face interviews were used with a response rate of about 80 percent across all years. The principal investigator responsible for the Election Study of 1968 was Bo Särlvik. The Election Studies of 1985, 1988, and 1994 have been directed by Mikael Gilljam and Sören Holmberg.

The Swedish Election Studies starting back in 1956 are deposited at The Swedish Social Science Data Service (SSD) at Göteborg University and are available to all interested scholars. The Riksdag surveys, however, are not deposited at any archive. The reason being difficulties in guaranteeing anonymity for the individual respondents in the Riksdag. Scholars interested in doing analysis on the Riksdag surveys will have to contact Peter Esaiasson or Sören Holmberg.

In the book, 37 different Swedish issue questions were used in the analyses. In Table 1 all these issue questions are listed. They were put to the members of the Riksdag as well as to eligible voters in the four Swedish Representation Studies. In the original Swedish studies there were some more issue areas covered.

More information in English about the Swedish Representation Studies and the Swedish Election Studies can be found in Esaiasson's and Holmberg's book *Representation from Above. Members of Parliament and Representative Democracy in Sweden* (1996) and in Holmberg's article *Election Studies the Swedish Way* (1994).

TABLE 1. Issue Questions put to members of parliament and to the general public in the Swedish Representation Study of 1968/69

Issue question	Number of response alternatives	Issue question	Number of response alternatives
Women in the work force	2	State-run companies	4
Public representatives on bank boards	2	Unemployment and government influence over banks and businesses	4
Lower taxes	2	Government control over private business	4
Religious teaching in schools	2	Private business without state interference	4
Movie censorship	3	Decrease social benefits	4
Abortion	4	More social reforms	4
Foreign aid	3	No social benefits, except for the elderly and the disabled	4
Defense costs	3		
EEC membership	2	Too much equality in Sweden	4
Agriculture support	2	More income equality	4
Commercial TV	2		
		Total number of issue questions	20

Appendix

TABLE 2. Issue Questions put to members of parliament and to the general public in the Swedish Representation Studies of 1985, 1988, and 1994

Issue question	Number of response alternatives	1985	1988	1994
Reduce the public sector	5	x	x	x
Dismantle the wage earner funds	5	x		
Reduce defense spending	5	x	x	x
More privately run health care	5	x	x	x
Forbid all pornography 5		x	x	x
Allow commercials on TV	5	x	x	
Build more day care centers	5	x	x	
Introduce a six-hour work day	5	x	x	x
Retain nuclear power	5	x	x	x
Reduce income differences	5		x	x
Ban inner-city driving	5		x	x
EU membership	5		x	
Increased gasoline tax to improve the environment	5		x	
Increase taxes on high incomes	5			x
Accept fewer refugees	5			x
Reduce the political influence of financial markets	5			x
Introduce gender-based affirmative action when recruiting higher civil servants	5			x
Total number of issue questions		9	12	12

Comment: The listed issue questions comprise all questions actually used in the empirical analysis reported in this book. In the original Swedish studies there were some more issue areas covered. The number of response alternatives for the issue questions do not include don't knows.

GERMAN REPRESENTATION STUDY 1988/89

The German data used in this book originate from one single study. Germany has seen only two representation studies so far: the study of Barbara G. Farah (1980) with data for 1970 which are unfortunately unavailable and the study of 1988/89. The German Representation Study 1988/89 consists of a study including a sample of eligible voters and the members of the German Bundestag. The study directed by Dietrich Herzog and Bernhard Wessels involved personal interviews on both levels, the voters and the members of parliament. The voters survey was a hook-up on the ZUMA Survey of the Social Sciences (ZUMA

Sozialwissenschaftenbus), coordinated by the Zentrum für Umfragen, Methoden und Analysen (ZUMA), Mannheim, and carried out by GFM-Getas. It includes standardized face-to-face interviews from 2009 respondents of the Federal Republic of Germany (West Gernany) including Berlin (West). The survey among the members of parliament was carried out by GfK Markforschung and includes personal interviews and a left-behing questionnaire for political career information. The response rate was 63,4 percent, i.e. 329 of 519 deputies. The study was financially supported by the German Science Foundation (DFG). Interviews were carried out between the second half of September 1988 and January 1989 in case of the members of parliament and from November to January in case of the voters survey.

The data are archived at the Zentralarchiv für empirische Sozialforschung, Köln (ZA). However, access is restricted in order to guarantee the anonymity for the individual respondents of the Bundestag.

From the information available in the surveys about issues and values, linkages, roles, expectations and how representation do and should work, only information on issues and values have been used in the book This includes the position on eleven issues and left-right self-placement.

More information about the German Representation Study can be found in: Herzog, Rebenstorf, Werner, Wessels, *Abgeordnete und Bürger* (1990) and in Herzog, Rebenstorf, Wessels (eds.), *Parlament und Gesellschaft* (1993).

Issue Questions put to members of parliament and to the general public in the German Representation Study 1988/89

Issue Questions	Number of Response Alternatives
Continuation of economic growth and technical progress	5
More say for people in political decision-making	5
Strengthen public custodians of the law	5
Restrict the right to demonstrate	5
Environmental protection should be considered in economic and political decision-making	5
Abortion should be facilitated	5
There should be less competition and pressure among the people	5
Political parties should have less, citizens' initiatives more influence	5
Secure supply of energy also with nuclear power	5
More influence for trade unions	5
Who wants to work should be guaranteed an appropriate job	5
Left-Right self-placement	10

Index